This is a continuation in the series of publications produced by the Center for Advanced Concepts and Technology (ACT), which was created as a "skunk works" with funding provided by the CCRP under the auspices of the Assistant Secretary of Defense (NII). This program has demonstrated the importance of having a research program focused on the national security implications of the Information Age. It develops the theoretical foundations to provide DoD with information superiority and highlights the importance of active outreach and dissemination initiatives designed to acquaint senior military personnel and civilians with these emerging issues. The CCRP Publication Series is a key element of this effort.

Check our Web site for the latest CCRP activities and publications.

www.dodccrp.org

DoD Command and Control Research Program

Assistant Secretary of Defense (NII)
&
Chief Information Officer
John G. Grimes

Principal Deputy Assistant Secretary of Defense (NII)
Dr. Linton Wells, II

Special Assistant to the ASD(NII)
&
Director of Research
Dr. David S. Alberts

Library of Congress Cataloging-in-Publication Data

Kass, Richard A.
  The logic of warfighting experiments / Richard A. Kass.
    p. cm. -- (The future of command and control)
  "DoD Command and Control Research Program."
  Includes bibliographical references and index.
  ISBN 1-893723-19-4
  1. Military research--United States--Field work. 2. Command and
control systems--United States. 3. United States--Armed Forces--
Reorganization--Methodology. 4. War games--United States. I. Title. II.
Series.
Editing, illustrations, and cover by Joseph Lewis
  U393.5.K37 2006
  355'.07--dc22
                                                    2006024433
August 2006

The Future of Command and Control

THE
LOGIC
OF
WARFIGHTING
EXPERIMENTS

RICHARD A. KASS

For the past 7 years, Dr. Rick Kass has served as Chief of Analysis for the Joint Experimentation Directorate in U.S. Joint Forces Command (JFCOM). Prior to this, Dr. Kass spent 18 years designing and analyzing operational tests for the U.S. Army Test and Evaluation Command. The methodology and procedures described in this book do not represent the official policy of Joint Forces Command or any U.S. Agency.

TABLE OF CONTENTS

LIST OF FIGURES

PREFACE

Military transformation is about change. Transformation decisions rest on the proposition that developing better military capabilities will produce or cause better military effects. Experimentation is uniquely suited to support transformation decisions. Experimentation involves changing something and observing the effects so that we can reach conclusions about cause and effect. Experimentation is the preferred scientific method for determining causality.

Experimentation has proven itself in science and technology, yielding dramatic advances. Can we apply the same experiment methods to the military transformation process? Can the same experiment methods achieve similar advances in military effectiveness? The thesis of this book is that robust experimentation methods from the sciences can be adapted and applied to military experimentation and will provide the foundation for continual advancement in military effectiveness.

In its simplest formulation, *to experiment* is *to try.* In this sense, experimentation is a characteristic of human nature and has existed from earliest times. When early humans attempted different ways to chip stone into cutting edges or selected seeds to grow sturdier crops, they were experimenting. When we try different routes to work to save commuting time or apply alternative rewards to get our kids to study more, we are experimenting. Militaries have always experimented with *potential causes* to enhance *effects*; whether it was sharper-edged swords, projectiles delivered by gunpowder, ironclad ships, or nuclear weapons.

Warfighting experiments are experiments conducted to support the development of operational military concepts and capabilities. Military concepts focus on *ways* to conduct military operations while capabilities focus on the *means* to execute the concepts. Warfighting experiments belong to *applied* rather than *pure* research; they are often executed in field or operational settings rather than in the laboratory. These experiments include human participants, usually military personnel, rather than animal, plant, or physical elements in the experiment.

There are excellent graduate-level books on the application of general scientific experimentation techniques for disciplines such as physics, chemistry, engineering, biology, medicine, sociology, and psychology. This book focuses on the application of experimentation techniques to warfighting experiments.

This book has three purposes. The first is to show that there is an inherent logic and coherence to experimentation when experimentation is understood as the pursuit of cause and effect. The second purpose is to illustrate that this logic is easy to understand and extremely useful when designing experiments to support the capability development process.

The third purpose is to present a framework derived from this logic to organize "best practices" and provide a rationale for considering tradeoffs among these techniques in the design of experiments.

Defense experimentation agencies need to provide credible experiment results. This is often communicated as a requirement for increasing experiment "rigor." What is meant by experiment rigor? To some, rigor means more realistic scenarios with better portrayals of an unrestrictive and adaptive threat; to others it means more quantitative data; and to still others it means examining fewer variables under more controlled conditions. Experiment rigor includes all of these and more. Defense experimentation agencies have developed lists of lessons learned or best practices to increase experiment rigor. These lists are compendiums of good experiment techniques (dos and don'ts) developed by experienced practitioners. What these lists lack is a logical framework based on an explicit concept of experiment validity. This book provides that framework.

A logical framework that organizes good experiment practices must provide four benefits:

- The framework needs to be based on a construct of experiment validity to show how individual experiment techniques contribute to experiment validity.
- It should be grounded on a few primary logical requirements to organize a large number of currently identified diverse good practices from sample size considerations to participant training.
- The framework needs to show the interrelationships among this multitude of good practices. We know that

some experiment techniques are mutually exclusive. For example, a common good technique is to conduct experiment trials under similar conditions while varying only the primary treatment variable to control the extraneous variable. Unfortunately, this works against the good experiment practice of allowing an independent free-play adversary to challenge the Blue force in each trial. So when is it best to control and when is it best to allow free play? The framework for organizing experiment techniques needs to assist the experimenter in making intelligent tradeoffs among good practices when designing individual experiments.

• Finally, the framework needs to provide a rationale and roadmap to develop experiment campaigns such that the limitations in any single experiment can be overcome by developing a series of related experiments in an experiment campaign that accumulates validity to support the final conclusions.

No framework can be exhaustive. An experiment framework should provide the foundation rationale for continuously developing additional good experiment techniques. While many examples of good experiment techniques are provided in this book, understanding the logical basis for these good techniques is more important than the list of techniques themselves. This will allow the experimenter "on the ground" to be creative in finding innovative methods for countering specific threats to experiment validity. Current lists of good practices by experienced practitioners can be used to augment the techniques provided in this book. This framework anticipates that good techniques for experimentation will continue to evolve and be incorporated into this logical framework.

Like many other authors have stated, "if this book advances the vision of experimentation, it is because I am standing on the shoulders of giants." Donald Campbell of Northwestern University and his colleagues Donald Cook, Julian Stanley, and William Shadish have investigated and written about the application of experiment techniques to the field setting for over 40 years. I first became acquainted with their book *Quasi-experimentation: Design and Analysis Issues for Field Settings* in graduate school in 1979 and used it as my primary reference to design military operational tests and experiments for 22 years until they published *Experimental and Quasi-Experimental Designs for Generalized Causal Inference* in 2002. My book is essentially a translation of their ideas applied to warfighting experimentation. In this translation process I have taken the liberty to rearrange, supplement, and rename many of their original ideas to adapt them to general military terminology and specific issues in warfighting experimentation. But this book would not be possible without their shoulders to stand upon. Any mistakes or misunderstanding in the translation process are mine.

I owe a debt of gratitude to Dr. Richard E. Hayes, who has done more than anyone I know to improve measurement, testing, and experimentation techniques for the military command and control process. I first met Dick in 1989 when he trained me as a data collector to provide quantitative command and control data in a field test. I also want to thank my co-workers and mentors during my 25-year career in military testing and experimentation. This book is a compilation of what I learned from them. And finally, a special appreciation to my wife Cheryl for spending countless hours proof-reading multiple early renditions.

Portions of this book have appeared in earlier publications. Key material has been published as a stand-alone pamphlet by the U.S. Joint Forces Command in 2004 and also appears in a North Atlantic Treaty Organization (NATO) Research and Technology Organization (RTO) Studies and Simulation (SAS) Symposium Report (2005). Earlier versions of the ideas in Chapters 2 through 8 were published in various sections in The Technical Cooperation Program (TTCP) *Guide to Understanding and Implementing Defense Experimentation (GUIDEX, 2006)*.

CHAPTER 1

INTRODUCTION

EXPERIMENTS AND MILITARY TRANSFORMATION

Increasingly, the United States and other NATO nations employ experimentation to assist in developing their future military capabilities. The United States Department of Defense (DOD) stresses the importance of experimentation as the process that will determine how best to optimize the effectiveness of its joint force to achieve its vision of the future.[1] An experimentation strategy is the cornerstone of the U.S. transformation strategy.[2]

> Joint experimentation—unconstrained in scope and devoted to defining military structures, organizations, and operational approaches that offer the best prom-

---

[1] The Joint Staff. *Joint Vision 2020*. Washington, DC: U.S. Government Printing Office. June 2000. p. 34.

[2] *Quadrennial Defense Review (QDR) Report: 2001*. September 2001. p. 35.

ise from new technology—joins [with] joint standing forces as the most efficient, effective, and expeditious means of designing the future in parallel with improving the ability to fight jointly.[3]

Further evidence of the importance of experimentation is that DOD designated U.S. Joint Forces Command as the DOD executive agent for joint experimentation in 1998.

Why is experimentation vital to the military transformation process? The U.S. Secretary of Defense has written that transforming the U.S. military is essential to "defend our nation against the unknown, the uncertain, the unseen, and the unexpected."[4] Military transformation can be described quite broadly "as innovation on a grand scale, sufficient to bring about a discontinuous leap in military effectiveness."[5] On the other hand, others caution "revolutionary changes...should not be the sole focus of our transformational activities."[6] Whether transformational change occurs dramatically or incrementally, the key question is how does one decide what to change to transform the military?

Two essential attributes embedded in the idea of military transformation are the idea of change and the idea of cause

---

[3] Owens, Admiral William A., U.S. Navy (retired). "The Once and Future Revolution in Military Affairs." *Joint Forces Quarterly*. Summer 2002. p. 61.

[4] Rumsfeld, Donald H. "Transforming the Military." *Foreign Affairs*. May-June 2002. p. 3.

[5] Krepinevich, Andrew. "The Bush Administration's Call for Defense Transformation: A Congressional Guide." Washington, DC: Center for Strategic and Budgetary Assessments. 19 June 2001.

[6] Myers, General Richard B. "Understanding Transformation." Unpublished manuscript distributed electronically to students at the National War College. 3 December 2002. p. 4.

and effect. If something in the military is innovated (changed), then it will result in (cause) a change in military effectiveness. Correspondingly, the principal paradigm of experimentation is manipulating (changing) something and observing what happens.[7] When this manipulation is conducted under controlled conditions, conclusions about cause and effect can be made. Warfighting experimentation is especially suited to supporting decisions about change to effect transformation.

According to the DOD Office of Force Transformation, "successful defense experimentation must apply the scientific method in its transformation strategy."[8] Experimentation has proven itself in science and technology, yielding dramatic advances. Can the same experimentation methods be applied to the military transformation process? Can they achieve similar advances in military effectiveness?

Robust experimentation methods from the sciences can be adapted and applied to military experimentation and will provide the foundation for continual advancement in military effectiveness.

While this book focuses on the utility of experimentation to support military transformation, one should not discount the role of military experts and operational lessons learned. Military experts offer a wealth of knowledge to support transformation. However, sometimes experts do not agree on what the best approach should be; and sometimes the expert answer may not be the best. For example, most experts ini-

---

[7] From Richard P. Feynman's description of science in *The Meaning of It All: Thoughts of a Citizen Scientist.* Helix Books. 1998.

[8] Cebrowski, Arthur K. "Criteria for Successful Experimentation." Memorandum for Secretaries of Military Departments. 7 July 2003. p. 1.

tially agreed that aircraft carriers should be used for long-range surveillance to support battleship tactics. It took operational experience in World War II to teach them differently. Warfighting experiments can examine employment alternatives in multiple scenarios before going to war and let the experiment data show which alternative is most effective.

Operational lessons learned are critical to identifying how particular warfighting capabilities were organized, equipped, and employed during specific operations. Lessons learned will also identify the results of military engagements, the number of targets engaged, ordnance expended, casualties, and so on. Lessons learned analysis, however, can only speculate on which capabilities accounted for which effects. In a complex military operation, it is seldom clear exactly why some aspects went well and some did not. This is problematic for transformation when one is interested in deciding which capabilities need to be continued and which deficiencies need to be remedied. Warfighting experimentation, by its nature, is designed to take this information and systematically sort through the cause-and-effect relationships, thereby lending science to the lessons learned transformation process.

EXPERIMENTS AND THE CONCEPT AND PROTOTYPE DEVELOPMENT PROCESS

Experiments are required throughout the concept development and prototyping process (Figure 1). They provide an empirical method to explore new capabilities to refine concepts and to validate new prototypes for joint force implementation. During the discovery phase, multinational military experts review current operational lessons and apply the lessons of military history to clarify the future environment.

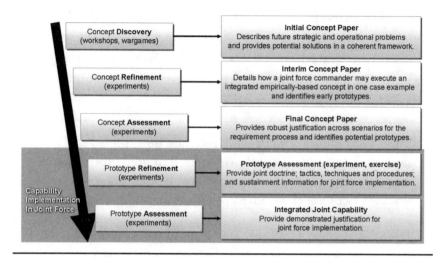

Figure 1. Concepts and Prototyping Process

Through conferences and seminar-type wargames, these experts, along with experts from academia and industry, identify future capabilities that may provide solutions to future uncertainties. Sometimes early experiments are conducted during the discovery phase to examine hypothetical scenarios to obtain a more comprehensive examination of potential future problems and solutions. An initial concept paper summarizes the future operational problem and proposed capability solutions within a conceptual framework.

During concept refinement, experiments quantify the extent to which proposed capabilities solve military problems. Experiments also examine capability redundancies and tradeoffs and reveal capability gaps. Prior discovery phase activities only speculate whether proposed future capabilities would solve identified gaps in military effectiveness. Refinement experimentation empirically substantiates and quantifies the extent that proposed capabilities increase effectiveness. The concept paper now provides a refined description of the future operational environment and provides an empirical basis for a reduced, integrated set of capabilities based on a particular example. In some instances, experimentation may suggest prototypes for early implementation.

Joint Warfighting Doctrine: Describes how the joint force fights today; "fundamental principles that guide the employment of forces of two or more Services in coordinated actions towards a common objective." (Joint Publication 1-02)

Joint Warfighting Concept: Describes how the joint force will employ future capabilities to fight in the future.

Joint Warfighting Capability: The ability to achieve a desired effect under specified standards and conditions through combinations of means and ways to perform a set of tasks.

Joint Warfighting Prototype: An initial working model of a capability designed to support operational concepts or operational requirements and may consist of people, processes, and technology.

Joint Warfighting Experiment: To explore the effects of manipulating proposed joint warfighting capabilities or conditions.

Concept assessment experiments investigate the robustness of the solution developed during refinement for possible future military operations. These experiments examine the concept under different future contingencies, different multinational environments, and different threat scenarios to ensure that the refinement phase solution is applicable to a wide range of potential operational requirements in an uncertain future. Results from this phase provide the justification for concept acceptance and prototype identification for eventual implementation.

Prototypes derived from concept capabilities are often not ready for immediate operational use. Prototype refinement experiments transition concept surrogates into potential operational joint capabilities by developing complete prototype packages for combatant commands. Refinement experiments develop the detailed tactics, techniques, and procedures (TTPs), and organizational structures for the prototype as well as develop the tasks, conditions, and standards to facilitate joint training. These experiments also examine the latest hardware and software solutions and their interoperability with existing fielded systems. Refinement experiments develop early prototypes for transition into combatant commanders' operational forces.

After progressing through the prior stages, prototype assessment experiments provide demonstrated evidence to the combatant commander that the prototype capability can operate within his theater and will improve his joint operations. Often these experiments are embedded within joint exercises or joint events and are used to validate the predicted gains in effectiveness of the joint force.

THE APPROACH IN THIS BOOK

Chapter 2 discusses the nature of an experiment and experiment validity and provides definitions of both.

Chapter 3 examines the logic of experimentation. This logic, based on the mnemonic "2, 3, 4, 5, 21," shows how all parts of the experiment process—hypothesis, experiment components, experiment requirements, and associated threats to validity—are related in the concept of cause and effect.

Chapters 4, 5, 6, and 7 present each of the four experiment requirements in detail. Meeting these four requirements is the essence of designing valid experiments and coherent experiment campaigns. Across these four chapters, 21 threats that impede the ability to meet the four requirements are enumerated. The primary focus of each chapter is a discussion of experiment techniques to counter these 21 threats to experiment validity.

Chapter 8 presents the application of the experiment logic and good practices to the design of an individual experiment. All experiments are a compromise and I present the notion of experiment tradeoffs among the four experiment requirements and associated good techniques in designing an individual experiment.

Chapter 9 discusses the art of designing experiments with multiple trials. These experiment designs involve the use of baselines or comparisons of multiple capabilities. Nine prototypical designs are illustrated and examined with respect to their ability to meet the four experiment requirements.

Chapter 10 extends the application of this logical framework to the construction of integrated experiment campaigns. Experiment campaigns should be designed so that deficiencies in any one experiment are overcome in succeeding experiments during the course of the experiment campaign.

Appendix A summarizes the many experiment techniques discussed in Chapters 4, 5, 6, and 7. This summary in its abbreviated format is useful as a handy reference.

Appendix B employs the experiment logic to explain the similarities and differences among related activities: tests, training, and demonstrations.

HOW TO USE THIS BOOK

Military and civilian managers interested in an executive summary or overview should read Chapters 1 and 2. This chapter discusses the role of experimentation in transformation while Chapter 2 summarizes the primary principles of experimentation that are explained in more detail in Chapters 4 through 10.

Experiment practitioners and analysts involved in the design, execution, and reporting of experiments will profit from the detail exposition of the logic of experimentation in Chapter 3 and its implications for designing better experiments in the remaining chapters. Those with a background in test and evaluation will find the discussion in Appendix B helpful for relating these experimentation guidelines to the testing arena.

This is not a book about experiment *statistics*. It is a book about the *logic* of experiment design—a framework for understanding the validity implications of designing experiments. Occasionally the text will make references to statistical terms such as analysis of variance (ANOVA), analysis of covariance (ANCOVA), degrees of freedom, and advanced experiment designs such as factorial designs or the use of blocking factors. Not all readers will be familiar with these terms. They are included to provide more advanced readers with connections between this logic framework and traditional experiment statistic topics and directions for further investigations.

INSPIRATION FOR THIS BOOK

The presentation of this logical framework for understanding warfighting experiments—the idea of a hierarchy of four experiment requirements, the threats to validity, and the experiment techniques to address these threats—is adapted from over 40 years of investigations by Donald Campbell, Donald Cook, Julian Stanley, and William Shadish in three seminal works:

William R. Shadish, Thomas D. Cook, and Donald T. Campbell. *Experimental and Quasi-Experimental Designs for Generalized Causal Inference.* (Boston: Houghton Mifflin Company, 2002).

Thomas D. Cook and Donald T. Campbell. *Quasi-Experimentation: Designs and Analysis Issues for Field Settings.* (Chicago: Rand-McNally, 1979).

Donald T. Campbell and Julian C. Stanley. *Experimental and Quasi-experimental Designs for Research.* (Chicago: Rand-McNally, 1963).

Their work is the best treatise on how to apply scientific experimentation techniques to the non-laboratory field setting. Their insights culminate over 40 years of thinking about experiment validity, the threats to validity, and techniques for combating these threats. These insights are the foundation for the presentation in this book. I have modified some of their ideas and language to make it more readily useful to non-expert practitioners who are often involved in warfighting experiments. Notwithstanding my adaptations, modifications, possible misunderstandings, and perhaps even some distortions of their ideas, the following presentations in this book would not have been possible without their work.

CHAPTER 2

WHAT IS AN EXPERIMENT?

I n 400 B.C., philosophers Socrates, Plato, and Aristotle investigated the meaning of knowledge and the methods to obtain it, using a *rational-deductive* process (Figure 2). Later, scientists Ptolemy and Copernicus developed *empirical-inductive* methods that focused on precise observations and explanation of the stars. These early scientists were not experimenters. It is only when later scientists began to investigate earthly objects rather than the heavens,that they uncovered a new paradigm for increasing knowledge.

In the early 1600s, Francis Bacon[9] introduced the term *experiment* and Galileo conducted experiments by rolling balls down

---

[9] "There remains simple experience which, if taken as it comes, is called accident; if sought for, *experiment*....the true method of experience....commencing as it does with experience duly ordered and digested, not bungling or erratic, and from it educing axioms, and from established axioms again new *experiments*....a method rightly ordered leads by an unbroken route through the woods of experience to the open ground of axioms."[Italics added] Bacon, Francis. *Novum Organum*. Section 82. 1620.

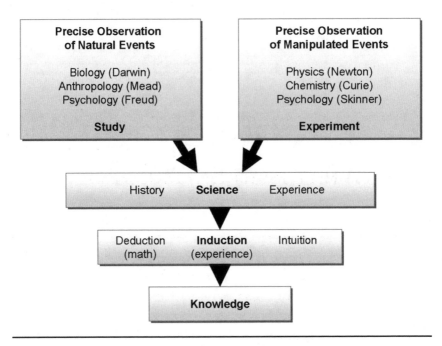

Figure 2. Taxonomy of Knowledge

an inclined plane to describe bodies in motion. The realization that manipulating objects would yield knowledge spawned a new research paradigm, one unimagined in the previous 2,000 years of exploring the out-of-reach heavens. The basis of this new science paradigm called *experimentation* was a simple question: "If I do this, what will happen?"[10] The key to understanding experimentation, and the characteristic that separates experimentation from all other research methods, is manipulating something to see what happens. The scientific aspect of experimentation is the manipulation of objects under controlled conditions while taking precise measurements. In its

[10] From Richard P. Feynman's description of science in *The Meaning of It All: Thoughts of a Citizen Scientist.* Helix Books. 1998.

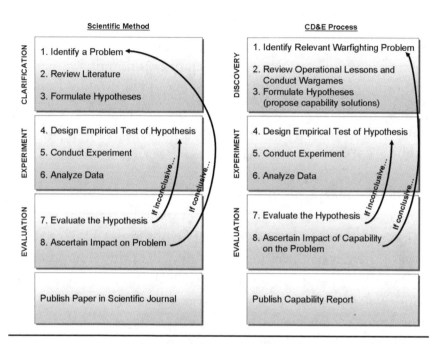

Figure 3. The Scientific Method and Capability Development and Experimentation Process

simplest form, an experiment can be defined as a process *"to explore the effects of manipulating a variable."*[11]

EXPERIMENTS AND THE SCIENTIFIC METHOD

The scientific method for experimentation has evolved over the past 400 years (Figure 3). The capability development and experimentation process (CDE) progresses through the same eight steps of that method. The process begins with discov-

---

[11] Shadish, William R., Thomas D. Cook, and Donald T. Campbell. *Experimental and Quasi-Experimental Designs for Generalized Causal Inference.* Boston, MA: Houghton Mifflin Company. 2002. p. 507.

ery—to clarify future warfighting problems and to seek
potential solutions. Current operational lessons learned,
defense planning guidance, combatant commands, wargames,
and other sources all help to identify and clarify initial operational problems. Similarly, military experts, wargames,
history, industry, and academia help to develop initial potential future solutions.

An initial concept summarizes the future operational environment, identifies impending operational problems, and
proposes solutions in the form of hypotheses. This concept
paper provides the basis for warfighting experimentation. If an
experiment result is inconclusive, such that one cannot determine if the original hypothesis was either supported or not
supported, then a better experiment is required. Conversely,
clearly positive or negative results provide an empirical basis to
refine and improve the concept.

CHARACTERISTICS OF AN EXPERIMENT

As experimentation expanded into the natural sciences of
astronomy, chemistry, and physics, early scientists began to
place more importance on observations of *manipulated* events
and the notion of control.[12] Control was necessary to keep elements out of their experiments that might inadvertently
influence the results, such as sterilizing test tubes before use to
keep out dust or bacteria. When experimentation moved into
the social domain of public health and education, controls
developed for the natural sciences in the laboratory environment did not work well in eliminating biases in the social

---

[12] Shadish et al., *Experimental and Quasi-Experimental Designs.* p. 2.

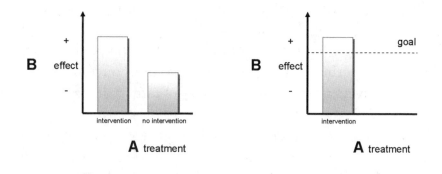

Figure 4. The Simplest Experiments

arena. Scientists developed new methods for experiments involving humans such as control groups and randomization.

Today, the key feature common to all experiments is still the deliberate variation of something so as to discover what happens to something else later—to discover the effects of presumed causes.[13]

The left-hand side of the Figure 4 displays the results of a simple experiment. It compares an intervention (manipulation) to a non-intervention. It is a side-by-side comparison that you might see your son or daughter propose for their school science fair. Your son or daughter plants two seeds in a box. He or she intervenes by adding fertilizer to the soil for one of the seeds and no fertilizer for the other seed. After watering both seeds regularly, they record and compare the height of both growing plants at some future date.

A comparable simple warfighting experiment might involve two player units. The experimenter "intervenes" by giving one

---

[13] Shadish et al., *Experimental and Quasi-Experimental Designs.* p. 3.

of the units a new capability, a new process or new equipment, and then observes both units as they execute a military task. The task might be detecting targets. At the completion of the task, the experimenter compares the two units on a measure of task effectiveness, such as the number of targets detected.

Occasionally, experiments do not involve side-by-side comparison (right-hand side of Figure 4). These simple experiments occur when there is a well-established threshold such that the results of an intervention can be compared to this threshold instead of comparison to an alternative condition. Sometimes pre-established thresholds are available from historical knowledge. For example, prior to 1947 no one had flown faster than the speed of sound. Experimental aircraft were flown to achieve this threshold rather than to out-perform some other aircraft. Pre-existing thresholds are also available in the military acquisition arena where a system must meet a specific threshold (for example, fire X rounds per minute) before the system will be funded. Experiments designed to compare a manipulation to a threshold are sometimes called *tests*. Appendix B discusses the similarities and differences between experiments and tests as commonly employed in the Department of Defense.

As can be seen from the seed example, the fundamentals of an experiment are not difficult to comprehend. So why do experimenters need academic training and books on "best practices"? The reason is that many questions can arise about an experiment that cast doubts on its conclusions. In the seed experiment, one could ask if the greater growth for the fertilized seed was really due to the fertilizer. Perhaps the fertilized seed was larger to start with, perhaps it had more sunlight, or perhaps the soil surrounding the seed was different from the soil around the unfertilized seed. Then again, perhaps the measurement of growth was incorrect. Should the experimenter measure growth from the top of the plant stem or from the height of the tallest leaf? Moreover, if there was no difference in growth between the fertilized and the unfertilized seed, would this mean that fertilizer does not work? It could alternately indicate that the experiment ended too soon and that fertilizer takes more time to work. Conversely, the lack of a difference could also indicate that the fertilizer worked better than expected and watering the plants distributed the fertilizer to the other plant's roots such that both plants profited from the fertilizer.

These questions cast doubt on any conclusion arising out of the seed experiment. Designing a good experiment, one that supports its conclusions, is a matter of eliminating the things that will cast doubt on the conclusions. An experiment that supports its conclusions is termed a *valid* experiment. Before discussing experiment validity, a formal definition of an experiment will be provided and the notion of cause and effect will be discussed.

DEFINITION OF A WARFIGHTING EXPERIMENT

Over 35 different definitions of *experiment* are available when conducting a web dictionary search.[14] Two common themes permeate these definitions: the notion of "doing something" and the notion of "new knowledge." Shadish, Cook, and Campbell provide a third theme in their 2003 monumental book *Experimental and Quasi-Experimental Designs for Generalized*

---

[14] OneLook Dictionary Search. http://www.onelook.com (May 2006)

Causal Inferences. They state that the purpose of an experiment is to ascertain the truth or falsity of a causal inference. Using the three themes of doing something, gaining knowledge, and the notion of cause and effect, more formal definitions of warfighting experiments can be offered.

According to Shadish, Cook, and Campbell (page 30) to *experiment is to explore the effects of manipulating a variable*. This definition captures the basic themes of gaining new knowledge *(explore)*, doing something *(manipulating a variable)*, and causality *(the effects)*. Based on their general definition, I propose the following derivatives for warfighting experimentation:

> Warfighting Experimentation: To explore the effects of manipulating proposed warfighting capabilities or conditions.

> Joint Warfighting Experimentation: To explore the effects of manipulating proposed joint warfighting capabilities or conditions.

CAUSE AND EFFECT IN WARFIGHTING EXPERIMENTS

Identifying experiments with the investigation of causality is a useful construct for understanding experiments. Causality is central to the transformation process. Military decisionmakers need to know what to change in order to improve military effectiveness. This is to say that the antecedent causes of effectiveness must be understood in order to change effectiveness. Effectiveness is improved by altering its antecedents, its causes.

The notion of cause and effect is inherent in the very language of an experiment and in the basic experiment paradigm "let's do this and see what happens." All warfighting innovation questions can be translated into a cause-and-effect question expressed as: "does A cause B?" Does the proposed military capability (A) produce (cause) an increase in warfighting effectiveness (B)? The idea of cause and effect is central to constructing the experiment hypothesis:

> If the unit uses the new capability (A),
> then it will increase its effectiveness (B).

The hypothesis is an expectation about A causing B. The definition of an experiment trial naturally follows. It is also wrapped in causality and derived from the hypothesis. An experiment trial is one presentation of the capability (A) to see if effect (B) occurred. Additional experiment trials might be the presentation of an alternative to capability A to see if effect (B) does not occur.

Explanations of warfighting experimentation sometimes miss the fundamental aspect of cause and effect as the unifying theme in experimentation.

> Today, the key feature common to all experiments is still to deliberately vary something so as to discover what happens to something later—to discover the effects of presumed causes.[15]

Because the notion of cause and effect is central to the discussion of experimentation in this book, it is worthwhile to pause

---

[15] Shadish et al., *Experimental and Quasi-Experimental Designs.* p. 3.

and explore the possibility of experimenting while unmindful of causality.

Try to imagine an attempt to design an experiment devoid of any interest in cause and effect. One might think of an example where an experimenter is unsure of the value of some new technology and is not sure how a military unit will use it. The experimenter gives the new technology to a player unit to "discover" what they do with it, to see if it helps them to do anything. The experimenter may also contend that they do not even have sufficient information to formulate a hypothesis: *If this capability, then what?*

After some consideration, however, they realize that contradictions abound in the idea of a "non-causal experiment." An experiment devoid of causality is counter to the central notion of experimenting: do something and see what happens. A non-causal experiment would indicate that the experimenter is interested in trying something new, but not interested in any results; or at least not interested in determining if any observed results were a result of the new technology. If the experimenter wants to conclude that any favorable results were a result of the new technology and not something else, then the experimenter has to enter the world of cause and effect. At the conclusion of the experiment, they will report that the new technology did or did not improve unit's performance, which is equivalent to stating that the technology did or did not cause an effect. It is difficult to conceive how one would report a useful conclusion of an experiment that did not involve cause and effect. One could only report something like the following:

In this experiment the unit used the new capability
and the unit accomplished task X; but we do not know

why the unit was able to accomplish the task. The unit may have accomplished the task even if they did not have the new capability.

Conducting an experiment without enough information to formulate a hypothesis is also a contradiction. A generic hypothesis might read as follows:

If the unit employs this new technology,
then they may be able to do task X better.

Is it possible that the experimenters would have no idea of what task or tasks to place in the "then" section of the hypotheses? This is almost never the case; and if it were true, the experiment would be a waste of time. If you gave experiment players something that the experimenter and the players truly had no idea how to use, they would not know whether to attempt to wear it, talk to it, float it, fly it, shoot with it, or eat it. The scientific process indicates that the experimenter must first do their homework. Through research and discussions with experts, the experimenter generates educated guesses on where the new technology might be useful and constructs plausible hypotheses.

EXPERIMENT RIGOR: EXPERIMENT VALIDITY

Defense experimentation agencies and senior-level decision-makers are appropriately concerned about credible experiment results. This is often communicated as a call for increasing "rigor" in the conduct of experiments. What is meant by *experiment rigor*? To some, increasing rigor means more realistic scenarios with better portrayals of unrestricted

and adaptive threats, while to others it means more quantitative data, and to still others it means examining fewer variables
under more controlled conditions. Experiment rigor includes
all of these and more. The focus of this book is experiment
rigor and how to increase it. This section defines experiment
rigor as experiment validity. Subsequent chapters will deal
with the logic and techniques to increase experiment rigor and
validity. To begin this journey, one must understand that
experiment validity is tied to the ability of the experiment to
connect cause and effect.

The strength of an experiment "is its ability to illuminate
causal inference."[16] This strength is what makes experiments
appropriate to address the underlying issue of transformation:
what capabilities are required to cause an increase in military
effectiveness in future warfare?

> How do we know if cause and effect are related? In a
> classic analysis formulated by the 19th-century philos-
> opher John Stuart Mill, a causal relationship exists if
> (1) the cause preceded the effect, (2) the cause is
> related to the effect, and (3) we can find no plausible
> alternative explanation for the effect other than the
> cause. These three characteristics mirror what hap-
> pens in experiments in which (1) we manipulate the
> presumed cause and observe an outcome afterwards,
> (2) we see whether variation in the cause is related to
> variation in the effect, and (3) we use various methods
> during the experiment to reduce the plausibility of
> other explanations for the effect.[17]

---

[16] Shadish et al., *Experimental and Quasi-Experimental Designs.* p. 18.
[17] Ibid., p. 6.

The term *valid* is an adjective.

> Valid: well-grounded or justifiable, being at once rele-
> vant and meaningful. logically correct.
> [Synonyms: sound, cogent, convincing, and telling.][18]
>
> Validity: "The truth of, correctness, or degree of sup-
> port for an inference."[19]

When these notions of validity are combined with the above
definition of an experiment, a definition of a well-designed
experiment is apparent:

> A well-designed experiment provides sufficient evi-
> dence to make a conclusion about the truth or falsity
> of the causal relationship between the manipulated
> variable and its effect.

Is a *well-designed experiment* the same as a *valid experiment*? Technically, no. Validity is a property of the conclusion of the
experiment, not the design of the experiment itself.[20] More
accurately, a shortened definition should read as follows:

> A well-designed experiment provides sufficient evi-
> dence to support a valid causal inference.

However, popular usage interchanges *well-designed* experiment
with *valid* experiment. Thus, one can say:

---

[18] Merriam-Webster Dictionary online. http://www.m-w.com (May 2006)

[19] Shadish et al., *Experimental and Quasi-Experimental Designs.* p. 513.

[20] Ibid., p. 34.

A valid experiment provides sufficient evidence to make a conclusion about the truth or falsity of the causal relationship between the manipulated variable and its effect.

In this book I will continue to use the popular term *valid experiment*, understanding that a valid experiment is a well-designed experiment that provides sufficient evidence for a valid conclusion.

Notice that the definition above uses the phrase "sufficient evidence." This is to reinforce the notion that the evidence is never absolute. All evidence, even in experimentation, retains some judgment. Chapter 8 will discuss the notion that there is no such thing as a perfect experiment and 100 percent validity certainty is unattainable. However, well-designed experiments can provide *sufficient* evidence to make a reasonable case for causality. The framework in this book presents four logical requirements to achieve sufficient validity in experiments to support causal inferences about capabilities and their effects.

Requirement 1: the ability to use the potential cause.

Requirement 2: the ability to observe an effect.

Requirement 3: the ability to isolate the reason for the observed effect.

Requirement 4: the ability to relate the results of the experiment to the real world.

The application of these requirements can be illustrated in the seed experiment above.

Requirement 1: Did the experimenter apply the fertilizer correctly?

Requirement 2: Did the experimenter observe a difference in the height between the two plants?

Requirement 3: Is the experimenter able to determine that any increase in height for the fertilized plant was due to the fertilizer and not something else?

Requirement 4: Finally, are the soil conditions in the experiment similar to those found in gardens to conclude that the results are applicable?

Can experiments fail? Yes, they can fail to provide sufficient evidence to determine whether the manipulated variable did (or did not) cause an effect. If the experimenter is unable to answer each of the four requirements in a positive manner, a meaningful conclusion is not possible about causality—the fertilizer did, or did not, produce increased growth.

The experimenter can fail to achieve any one of these four requirements because of known *threats to validity*.[21] These threats are the specific reasons we cannot achieve a particular experiment requirement. Experienced practitioners over the years have developed a number of experiment techniques or "good practices" to overcome these threats to validity. Chapters 4, 5, 6, and 7 present each of the four experiment-requirements in detail along with their threats and associated good techniques for ameliorating these threats.

---

[21] Shadish et al., *Experimental and Quasi-Experimental Designs.* p. 39.

DESIGNING RIGOROUS EXPERIMENTS

Designing warfighting experiments to meet each of the four experiment requirements is an art. A thorough understanding of the threats to the four requirements and the associated good experiment techniques is critical to applying good experiment techniques to eliminate or mitigate the threats to validity. Experimenters can never prove that they have designed a valid experiment. They can identify the potential threats to validity for their particular experiment and provide evidence that their experiment sufficiently controls or eliminates these threats so that the results will be interpretable and applicable to resolving the causal hypothesis under investigation.

It should be noted however, that all experiments are compromises. Resource costs have a major impact on experiment design and will always affect the ability to design a better experiment. A thorough understanding of the threats to validity and associated good practices is critical to optimizing experiment validity within resource constraints. Chapters 8, 9, and 10 will discuss tradeoffs in designing individual experiments or experiment campaigns to meet the four experiment requirements.

CHAPTER 3

EXPERIMENT LOGIC

"2, 3, 4, 5, 21" LOGIC

It has always been difficult to translate "design of experiments" textbooks into useful prescriptions for warfighting experiments, principally because warfighting experiments are constrained by time and resources, thus severely limiting the use of experiment control groups, multiple trials, and randomization of subjects to groups. These restrictions have led some to propose that warfighting experiments should operate from different principles than scientific experiments. Often this translates into a more relaxed set of principles, prompting a *laissez-faire* approach to designing warfighting experiments. When faced with constraints however, the solution is not to abandon basic experiment principles but to apply these principles in a rational, logical manner to accomplish experiment goals.

IF (treatment)...	THEN (effect)...
Independent variable	Dependent variable
Sea Basing	*Rapid deployment*
Collaboration	*Adaptive Planning*
Global Cell	*Inter-theater coordination*
Robust ISR	*Deny sanctuaries*

Figure 5. Two Parts to a Hypothesis

The key to the rational application of scientific experiment principles is understanding their logic within a heuristic framework. The logic of experimentation can be expressed as a mnemonic sequence of numbers: 2, 3, 4, 5, and 21. The following discussion illustrates that each number represents an aspect of a coherent logical framework that connects the essential characteristics of a warfighting experiment. Subsequent chapters will apply this framework to design more effective individual warfighting experiments and more effective experimentation campaigns.

2 | TWO PARTS IN AN EXPERIMENT HYPOTHESIS

The number "2" represents the two components of the hypothesis: the "If" side and the "Then" side (Figure 5). There are two ways to approach the experiment hypothesis. In most cases one has an operational problem that needs a solution. These operational problems are in the form of a requirement, such as the requirement to deploy forces more rapidly or the requirement to deny enemies the use of sanctuaries where they can rest and restore. In this instance, the Then side of the hypothesis is identified first and concept developers are in

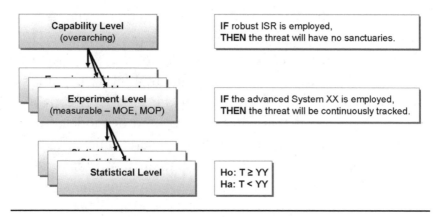

Figure 6. Levels of Hypothesis

search of possible solutions to place on the If side. When one or more solutions are developed, they are ready to express the If side of the hypotheses followed by the Then side expressing the potential resolution of the requirement: *If New Solution X is used, then Operational Problem Y might be solved.*

A second approach to hypothesis development is to begin with the left-hand side. This occurs when a new technology is available and experiments are conducted to determine whether the new technology has military applications. In this case, the new technology is the proposed solution and it is in search of a military problem to be solved or military tasks that can be enhanced. Often the technology sponsor offers ideas for possible applications. The hypothesis could be formulated as follows: *If New Technology X is employed, then Operational Tasks Y and Z will be enhanced.*

Levels of Hypotheses. It is useful to consider three different levels of warfighting experiment hypotheses (Figure 6). At the most abstract level the if-then aspects are described in terms of capabilities and operational effects. These capability hypotheses, however, are not useful to experimenters who require hypotheses with implementable treatments and observable effects. The high-level "capabilities hypothesis" needs to be translated into one or more "experimental level" hypotheses. This is accomplished by translating the high-level capability into *enabling* systems that can be surrogated or modeled in an experiment. These enabling systems include innovative technology, processes, or organizations. Similarly, the Then side of the high-level hypotheses is translated into specific strategic, operational, or tactical tasks to be accomplished along with associated measures of effectiveness (MOE) or measures of performance (MOP) for each task. From these experiment hypotheses, analysts develop associated statistical hypotheses to conduct statistical analyses of the data to determine whether the experiment results support the hypotheses at some level of statistical confidence.

Null Hypothesis. Sometime during the development of hypotheses, questions will arise concerning the *null hypothesis.* What is the null hypothesis and what is its role in the experiment process? The null hypothesis provides a statistical means to quantify the probability that a particular sample of data is derived from a hypothetical "parent" distribution. This technique can be described by way of example involving an experiment with a single group of 10 riflemen employing a new weapon. Prior to the experiment, these 10 riflemen are considered a representative sample from a hypothetical population of riflemen who use the current weapon. Historical data indicate the historical population of all riflemen with the current weapon score an average 250 points on the rifle range. Since this is an average, sometimes the riflemen with the current weapon scored higher and sometimes lower than the average. During the example experiment, the 10 riflemen achieve an average score of 275 with the new weapon, 25 points above the historic average.

The question is: does this experiment result represent only another variation from the original population, or does it represent a different, "improved" population? To answer this question, the analyst constructs a *null hypothesis* (Ho) that represents the situation if the *experiment treatment does not work*. That is, the new sample mean (M_{NS}), although higher than the historic average (M_H), still belongs to the historic population. This is written as Ho: $M_{NS} = M_H$. This translates as follows: the new-system average is less than,[22] or equal to, the historic average.

The *alternative hypothesis* (Ha) represents a more speculative, and currently non-existent, population that averages better than the null hypothesis population. It represents what a new population of riflemen will look like *if the new weapon is better*. That is, the new sample mean (M_{NS}), if higher than the historic average (M_H), belongs outside of the historic population. This is written as Ha: $M_{NS} > M_H$. This translates as follows: the new-system average is greater than the historic average.

At the conclusion of the experiment, statistical computations based on sample size, sample data results, and statistical risk assumptions will indicate whether or not the data support "rejecting the null hypothesis" in favor of the alternative hypothesis. If the statistical computational results are sufficient to reject the null hypothesis, by default the alternative hypothesis is accepted. The experimenter concludes that the treatment, the new system, is not just a variation of the old

---

[22] The "less than" is added to make the null hypothesis all inclusive, only excluding the alternative hypothesis.

population. Instead, the new system represents a new, improved population of rifleman.

The point of this technical discussion is that the null hypothesis is necessary to shape the statistical analysis of experiment data. It is less useful in communicating the higher level experiment hypotheses. By convention, the capability and experiment level hypotheses illustrated in Figure 6 are worded to reflect the *alternative hypothesis*, what happens *if the new capability works!* This is the best way to communicate the purpose of the experiment. The null hypothesis, the status quo, is unstated at the capability and experiment-level hypothesis because it is obvious, or at least implied; e.g. if the experiment capability does not work, the "threat *will continue* to have sanctuaries" and "the threat will *not* be continuously tracked." Statistical level hypotheses (bottom of Figure 6) require a precise formulation of the null (Ho) and alternative (Ha) hypotheses to support computational analysis of the experiment data to determine the probability that the data support either the Ho or Ha population conclusion.

Experiment Hypotheses in Training Exercises. The use of operational tasks for the Then portion of hypotheses is quite useful when experiments are conducted in conjunction with military training exercises. Many opportunities exist to explore new technologies and processes during exercises. The hypothesis associated with this type of experiment is a natural summary of what is proposed to result from the insertion of something different in the training exercise. Military training exercises are built around a series of tasks, conditions, and standards. In the joint training arena these are documented in the Uniform Joint Training List (UJTL). The task specifies what needs to be accomplished, the conditions provide the context, and the standards provide the measures of effectiveness. A capabilities level hypothesis suitable for an experiment embedded within a training exercise might follow the following format: *If the JTF staff employs new capability X, then Task Y will be enhanced.* The corresponding experimental hypothesis might be: *If the JTF staff employs system X, then Task Y will be accomplished in less time.* Chapter 8 discusses additional aspects of conducting experiments in military exercises.

Concerns about Hypotheses. A number of concerns have surfaced over the years about the use of hypotheses in warfighting experiments. These concerns take one or more of the following forms:

- There is not enough information to formulate hypotheses in early experiments.
- Hypotheses are too constrictive in early experiments and are thus detrimental to serendipitous discovery.
- Warfighting hypotheses are not justified because hypotheses are supposed to be derived from theory and there is no military theory.
- Hypotheses demand rigorous data and analysis, and warfighting data is not sufficient to accept or reject hypotheses.
- Hypotheses are not appropriate for messy field experiments; they are only useful in "controlled" experiments.

These concerns arise for several reasons. First, hypotheses are thought to be formal deductions derived from a scientific theory. This is a very narrow view of hypotheses. Few, even science experiments, are derived from formal scientific theories. Hypotheses are "educated guesses" or formulations of expectations to guide the experiment design. They are derived from homework, not theory. This pre-experiment homework is exemplified in the first two steps of the scientific method illustrated previously in Figure 3.

Second, it is mistakenly believed that hypotheses will prematurely narrow the experimenters' focus, obstructing the ability to seeing spontaneous, serendipitous results. All experimenters are trained to watch for unanticipated results. If we understand hypotheses as educated guesses, then we understand that they are only a starting point. Without hypotheses there is no expectation, and without expectation there can be no unanticipated findings. The key to serendipity is to be sensitive to the possibility of "finding unanticipated findings." Understanding that hypotheses are only educated guesses allows the experimenters to be open to the possibility that they could be wrong.

Finally, there is a perception that warfighting experiments can not be sufficiently rigorous to address hypotheses. Only laboratory experiments should have hypotheses. This book is a counter to this perception. All experiments, laboratory and non-laboratory experiments, fall short of the ideal. However, by understanding the logic of experiments, the four experiment requirements, their threats, and associated counter good practices, one can design warfighting experiments with sufficient validity to address causal hypotheses.

3 THREE LOGICAL STEPS TO RESOLVE HYPOTHESES

There are three components to resolving the conditional proposition contained in the hypothesis statement (Figure 7). The first logical question is whether the proposed solution, the left-hand side of the hypothesis, was adequately represented in the

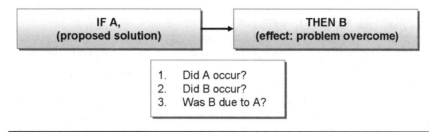

Figure 7. Three Steps to Resolving Hypotheses

experiment. This is not always easy to do given that new proposed solutions often involve surrogate software, hardware, and new procedures that are implemented for the first time for the experiment.

The second question is whether the experimenter was able to observe the right-hand side of the hypothesis. That is, did the experiment produce objective evidence that the problem to be solved was, in fact, solved?

Given that the proposed solution was represented and given that progress was observed in solving the problem, the third logical question concerns whether the observed problem resolution was due to the proposed solution. This third component of a hypothesis is the toughest challenge in warfighting experiments where so many alternative explanations of positive results exist. For example, the players with the proposed solution may have been better trained or more motivated.

4 FOUR REQUIREMENTS FOR A GOOD EXPERIMENT

What is a good experiment? How does one tell a good experiment from a bad experiment? The scientific term for a good

Hypothesis: If A, then B.

Requirement		Evidence for Validity	Threat to Validity
1	Ability to use the new capability.	A occurred.	The asset did not work or was not used.
2	Ability to detect change.	B changed as A changed.	Too much noise, cannot detect any change.
3	Ability to isolate the reason for the change.	A alone caused B.	Alternate explanations for the change are available.
4	Ability to relate results to actual operations.	Change in B due to A is expected in actual operations.	The observed change may not be applicable.

Figure 8. Four Requirements for a Good (Valid) Experiment

experiment is a "valid" experiment. Four logically sequenced requirements must be met to achieve a valid experiment (Figure 8). It should come as no surprise that the first three requirements reflect the three components of hypothesis resolution. This further reflects the centrality of the hypotheses to experiments. These three experiment requirements represent the *internal validity* of the experiment, the ability to determine whether a causal relationship exists between two variables.

The fourth requirement reflects the relevancy of the experiment to operations outside the experiment environment. This fourth requirement represents *external validity*, the ability to generalize the cause-and-effect relationship found in the experiment environment to the operational military environment. The four requirements represent a logical, progressive sequence within themselves. If each successive requirement is not met in sequence, there is no need to proceed to the next one.

A simple example will illustrate these four requirements. Suppose a proposed concept postulates that new sensors will be required to detect time critical targets. One experiment to examine this proposition might be a two-day military exercise in which the old array of sensors is employed on the first day and a new sensor suite is used on day two. The primary measure of effectiveness is the percent of targets detected. The hypothesis is: "If new sensors are employed, then time-critical target detections will increase." This experiment is designed to determine whether the new sensors (A) will cause an increase in detections (B).

1. Ability to Use the New Capability.

In most warfighting experiments, the majority of resources and effort are expended to bring the new experimental capability to the experiment. In the ideal experiment, the experimental capability (the new sensor) is employed by the experiment players to its optimal potential and allowed to succeed or not succeed on its own merits. Unfortunately, this ideal is rarely achieved in experiments. It is almost a truism that the principal lesson learned from the majority of experiments is that the new capability, not withstanding all of the expended effort, was not ready for the experiment.

There are a number of things that go wrong with experimental surrogate capabilities. The hardware or software does not perform as advertised. The experiment players are frequently undertrained and not fully familiar with its functionality. Because it is new, the techniques for optimum employment are not mature and will, by default, be developed by the experimental unit during the experiment trial. These threats and others to meeting the first experiment requirement will be discussed further in Chapter 4. If the experimental sensors (A) could not be functionally employed during the experiment, there is no reason to expect that they will affect the ability to detect targets (B) any greater than the current array of sensors.

2. Ability to Detect Change.

If the first experiment requirement is met and the sensors are effectively employed, then the transition from the old to the new sensors should be accompanied by a change in the number of detections observed. If this change in detections does not occur, the primary concern now is too much experimental noise. The ability to detect change is a signal-to-noise problem. Too much experimental error produces too much variability, making it difficult to detect a change. Many experiment techniques are designed to reduce experiment variation: calibrating instrumentation to reduce data collection variation, controlling stimuli (the targets) presentations to only one or two variations to reduce response (detections) variation, and controlling the external environment (time of day, visibility, etc.). Sample size is another consideration for reducing the signal-to-noise ratio. The computation of statistical error variability decreases as the number of observations increases. The threats to the ability to detect change and further details on attenuating these threats are the topic of Chapter 5.

3. Ability to Isolate the Reason for Change.

Let us suppose the experimenter met the first two requirements: the new array of sensors was effectively employed and the experimental design reduced variability and produced an observable change (increase) in the percent of detections. The question now is whether the detected change was due to the intended cause (changing from old sensors to new) or due to something else. The scientific term for alternate explanations of experimental data is *confounded results*. In this example, an alternate explanation for an increase in detections on day two is that it was due to a learning effect. The sensor operators may have been more adept at finding targets as a result of their experience with target presentations on day one and, consequently, would have increased target detections on day two whether the sensors were changed or not. This would dramatically change the conclusion of the detected change.

Scientists have developed experimental techniques to eliminate alternate explanations of the cause of change. These include counter-balancing the presentation of stimuli to the experimental unit, the use of placebos in drug research, use of a control group, randomizing participants between treatment groups, and elimination or control of external influencers. These techniques will be discussed more fully in Chapter 6.

4. Ability to Relate the Results to Actual Operations.

Again, let us suppose that the experiment was successful in employing the new capability, detecting change, and isolating the cause. Now the question is whether the experimental results are applicable to the operational forces in actual military operations. Experimental design issues supporting operational realism revolve around the representation of surrogate systems, the use of operational forces as the experimental unit, and the use of operational scenarios with a realistic reactive threat. More details on enhancing operational realism in order to extend experimental results to real operations are provided in Chapter 7.

Application of the Four Experiment Requirements

These four requirements for a good experiment are applicable to all experiments, whether conducted in a prestigious science lab, as a high school science project, or as warfighting experiments. Any experiment that produces clear evidence for or against a hypothesis is a success. If a new experimental capability does not live up to its expectations, as indicated by the hypothesis, it is not a failure for the experimentation process. However, experiments can fail. They can fail to provide the information necessary to resolve the hypothesis. There are three possible outcomes to every experiment: (1) the capability is effective, (2) the capability is not effective, and (3) unknown. A good experiment provides enough information to choose between 1 and 2. A failed experiment defaults to 3. If one still does not know whether the experimental capability is effective or not at the completion of the experiment, then the experiment failed. A failed experiment provides no information about proposed capability effectiveness. All that was learned was that the experiment was poorly designed.

The purpose of this book is to present the rationale for and examples of good scientific experimentation practices that can be applied to military experimentation. A good experiment is one that increases knowledge. A poorly constructed experiment is one that casts doubts on its findings, thus failing to increase our knowledge about the hypothesis. The only knowledge gained in a poor experiment is a better understanding of how to conduct a more valid experiment to meet the four experiment requirements.

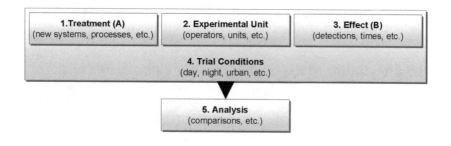

Figure 9. Five Experiment Components

5 FIVE COMPONENTS OF AN EXPERIMENT

All experiments—large or small, field or laboratory, military or academic, applied or pure—consist of five components[23] (Figure 9):

1. The *treatment*, the possible cause (A), is the proposed capability, the proposed solution that is expected to influence warfighting effectiveness.
2. The *experimental unit* executes the possible cause and produces an effect.
3. The possible *effect* (B) of the treatment is the result of the trial, an increase or decrease in some aspect of warfighting effectiveness.
4. The *trial* is one observation of the experimental unit under the treatment (A) or under the alternative (-A) to the new capability to see whether effect (B) occurred and includes all of the contextual conditions under which the experiment is executed.

---

[23] From: Cook, T.D. and Campbell, D.T. *Quasi-Experimentation: Design and Analysis Issues for Field Settings.* Rand McNally. 1979.

5. The *analysis* phase of the experiment compares the results from one trial to a different trial.

The first and third experiment components are bonded to the experiment hypothesis. The experiment treatment (A) represents the left-hand side of the hypothesis as the proposed solution, and the experiment effect (B) represents the right-hand side of the hypothesis as the problem to be overcome. The components of an experiment and hypothesis go hand in hand.

21 TWENTY-ONE THREATS TO A GOOD EXPERIMENT

How does one design a good or valid experiment? Too often validity is considered like art: "I can't explain it, but I know it when I see it." Questions about experiment validity are often answered by sending first-time experiment designers to the most experienced analyst to receive a list of dos and don'ts and lessons learned. The list of good practices often refers to the importance of sample size, realistic threats, representative units and operators, and so on. Many practical lists exist that admonish what should be done to design good warfighting experiments. In general, there is much overlap and agreement among various "codes of best practices" for experimentation. However, these lists do not show the interrelationships among the good practices and do not explicitly related individual practices to experiment validity.

It is possible to design a heuristic framework to organize good practices for designing valid experiments. The logic of experimentation has identified the four requirements for a good experiment. Things that can go wrong in an experiment are threats to validity (Figure 10)—problem areas that interfere

Experiment Components	Experiment Requirements				
	1. Ability to Use the Capability	2. Ability to Detect Change	3. Ability to Isolate the Reason for Change		4. Ability to Relate the Results to Operations
			Single Group	Multiple Groups	
1. Treatment	(1) Capability functionality does not work.	(5) Capability systems vary in performance.	(11) Functionality changes across trials.		(18) Functionality does not represent future capability.
2. Players	(2) Players are not adequately prepared.	(6) Experiment players vary in proficiency.	(12) Player proficiency changes across trials.	(15) Groups differ in player proficiency.	(19) Players do not represent operational unit.
3. Effect	(3) Measures are insensitive to capability impact.	(7) Data collection accuracy is inconsistent.	(13) Data collection accuracy changes across trials.	(16) Data collection accuracy differs for each group.	(20) Measures do not reflect important effects.
4. Trial	(4) Capability has no opportunity to perform.	(8) Trial conditions fluctuate.	(14) Trial conditions change across trials.	(17) Groups operate under different trial conditions.	(21) Scenario is not realistic.
5. Analysis		(9) Sample size is insufficient. (10) Statistical assumptions are violated.			

Figure 10. Twenty-One Threats to a Valid Experiment

with meeting any of the four experiment requirements. Experiment good practices are ways to eliminate, control, or ameliorate threats to validity. The framework proposed here identifies 21 threats[24] to warfighting experiments. These threats can be arranged within a two-dimensional matrix to better understand the actions the experimenter can take to counter these threats. In Figure 10, the 21 threats are arrayed with respect to the four experiment requirements and the five experiment components. The multitude of good experiment-design practices developed over the years to counter each of these 21 threats are presented in Chapters 4, 5, 6, and 7 and summarized in condensed form in Appendix A.

This framework organizes good experiment techniques as counters to the threats to the four experiment requirements. The framework makes it easier to understand why particular good practices are important and the impact on experiment validity if the threat is not properly countered. The framework will also be important in recognizing validity tradeoffs. As discussed later, it is impossible to counter all 21 threats in any particular experiment because some experiment techniques designed to counter one threat work against the experiment techniques designed to counter other threats. Thus, a thorough understanding of this framework is essential to designing the "best available" experiment. Practitioners will ultimately determine the value of this two-dimensional framework for thinking about and organizing experiment best practices.

---

[24] While Shadish, Cook, and Campbell identified 37 threats to validity, I have combined and distilled these down to 21 threats to warfighting experiments arranged into a two-dimensional matrix to illustrate how the threats to experiment validity can be understood and treated with respect to each of the four requirements and the five components of an experiment.

SUMMARY

Understanding the "2, 3, 4, 5, 21" logical framework of warfighting experimentation allows one to see the "big picture." It provides a rationale and road map for sorting through the myriad details encountered when designing experiments. Finally, the logic and resulting two-dimensional framework provides a coherent rationale for organizing experiment lessons learned and good practices as preventable threats to validity to increase the scientific rigor of warfighting experiments.

Experiments are essential to developing an empirically based transformation process. New capabilities include the doctrine, organization, training, materiel, leadership, personnel, and facilities that will enable or cause future warfighting effectiveness. Experimentation is the preferred scientific method for establishing whether hypothesized capabilities are causally related to effects. If the five experiment components are designed to meet the four experiment requirements, the experiment will provide the concept developer with the basis to proceed. Application of these scientific principles ensures that new warfighting capabilities will be empirically related to warfighting effectiveness, thus providing the foundation for transforming military forces.

Designing warfighting experiments to meet each of the four experiment requirements is an art. The next four chapters discuss the 21 threats to validity associated with each of the four experiment requirements.[25] A thorough understanding of the 21 threats and the associated good experiment techniques is critical to knowing what tradeoffs are required in the application of experiment techniques.

Tradeoffs are required in experiment design. First, resource costs will always impact the ability to design a better experiment. A thorough understanding of the threats to validity and associated good practices is critical to optimizing experiment validity within resource constraints. Secondly, different experiment practices often work against one another. For example, one good technique is to have multiple similar trials, called *rep-*

---

[25] The material in Chapters 5, 6, 7, and 8 on experiment requirements, the threats to validity, and the experiment techniques to address these threats is adapted from: Shadish et al., *Experimental and Quasi-Experimental Designs*. Their work serves as the foundation for the following discussion, although several changes to their presentation are introduced here. Much of their original terminology has been translated into military terminology, for example their "maturation effects" is translated as "learning effects" and all examples of good experiment practices are in regards to military warfighting experiments. Additionally, two of their original four requirements (construct validity and external validity) are combined into a single external validity Requirement 4, the ability to relate results. In warfighting experimentation most effects of interest are straightforward (detections, engagements, etc.) and there is far less emphasis on constructs. And finally, the discussion of Requirement 1, ability to use the capability, is not considered as one of their original four validity requirements. They discuss it as a "special problem" of experiment treatment implementation. It is elevated here as Requirement 1 because it is consistent with the logic of experimentation (the left-hand side of the hypothesis) and because it is such a prevalent problem in warfighting experiments. Notwithstanding these adaptations to Shadish, Cook, and Campbell's validity framework, the following discussion would not have been possible without their book, which culminates 40 years of investigating experiment validity in non-laboratory settings.

lications, to increase statistical rigor. However, constructing similar trials where the Red players operate the same way in successive trials works against the good practice of ensuring independent Red player actions during each trial to increase realism. A thorough discussion of the tradeoffs among the four requirements will be discussed in Chapters 8, 9, and 10 when designing individual experiments or experiment campaigns.

Chapter 4

Experiment Requirement 1:
Ability to Use the New Capability

Some of the most frustrating and, unfortunately, most consistent lessons learned from warfighting experiments are the following:

- The proposed capability did not work as well as promised.
- The players did not know how to use the new capability properly.
- The experiment scenario was not sufficiently sensitive to the new capability.
- The experiment trial did not give the players the opportunity to use the new capability.

These experiment lessons are most frustrating because, in most cases, the majority of pre-experiment resources and efforts are expended toward developing and getting the new

Experiment Component	Threat
Treatment	(1) Capability functionality does not work.
Player	(2) Players are not adequately prepared.
Effect	(3) Measures are insensitive to capability impact.
Trial	(4) Capability has no opportunity to perform.

Figure 11. Threats to the Ability to Use the New Capability

experimental capability to the experiment. Ensuring that the experimental capabilities can make a difference in the experiment outcome is the first logical step in designing a valid warfighting experiment. The first four threats to experiment validity (Figure 11) indicate the things that can go wrong when attempting to employ a new experimental capability in an experiment.

THREATS TO REQUIREMENT 1

Threat 1. New capability functionality does not work.

The most frequent threat to Requirement 1 is that the experimental hardware or software does not work as advertised. Experiment players will attempt to make just about anything work but they cannot overcome deficiencies in basic system functionality. One of the major corollaries to this threat in the command, control, and communications area is interoperability. Systems that interoperated in the designer's facility almost surely will not interoperate when initially brought to the experiment. Good experiment practices to alleviate this threat are obvious but challenging nonetheless. The experiment director needs to schedule frequent demonstrations of the new capability's functionality and interoperability prior to the experiment.

These demonstrations should include pilot tests in the environment of the experiment with all other systems when possible.

Threat 2. Experiment players are not adequately prepared to use the new capability to its fullest extent.

The second most prevalent threat to Requirement 1 is that the experiment players are often under-trained and not fully familiar with new capability's functionality. This frequently occurs because the new system is not available for training until the last minute. On those rare occasions when the system is available, it is not fully functional (Threat 1). Thus, a five-day pre-experiment training period turns into four days of lectures about the system's functionality and hands-on practice with an incomplete system on the last day of scheduled training. Even when the system is available, new equipment training tends to focus on operator skills rather than employment techniques because the tactics, techniques, and procedures for optimum employment are non-existent or immature. Too often the TTPs are developed by the experimental unit during the early experiment trials. Similarly, for new and complex staff-support systems the standard operating procedures (SOPs) are not developed. So while the operators may be trained on their operational role with the new processes, the procedures for receiving inputs and providing and incorporating the outputs of a new process will falter.

Once again the good practices are obvious, especially in the military where training is an integral aspect of the everyday mission. The key is to anticipate the problems identified above and provide sufficient practice time for players to be able to operate and optimally employ the system. This means that not only do the new functionality and interoperability need to be available and thoroughly tested prior to experimental unit training, but also that the TTPs and SOPs have to be developed concurrently with the new capability development. This is not an easy task when developing procedures for a capability that does not yet exist in its final form.

Threat 3. Experiment measures are insensitive to new capability impact.

While the previous two threats are generally acknowledged and the associated good practices are well-established, Threat 3 often falls below the horizon. Threat 3 identifies the need to ask oneself: "If this system is used to its fullest extent, will it make a noticeable difference on the outcome measures: measures of effectiveness (MOE) and measures of performance (MOP)?" Are the measures sensitive to its potential impact? Several good practices ameliorate this threat.

Pilot tests or full-dress rehearsals prior to the start of experiment trials not only provide a check on Threats 1 and 2, but are also the best way to counter Threat 3. The experimenter should examine the trial environment to see if it is structured to give the new capability a fair chance to demonstrate its advertised strengths on the outcome measures. If the experiment is to be a comparison between the old and new capabilities, it is critical to include the old capability in the pilot test. It is always a good idea to structure some experiment trials where it is expected that the old system may perform equivalent to the new capability and structure other experiment trials where the advantages of the new capability should allow it to excel. These trials should be examined during the pilot test to test these assumptions.

If one does not see indications of performance differences between the old and new capabilities during the pilot test, the trial scenario should be re-examined. Perhaps the scenario does not sufficiently emphasize the operational envelope of the new capability. Otherwise, it may not be worthwhile to continue into the experiment trials.

If the experiment is to examine different levels of a capability, then it must increase the difference between the treatment levels to increase the chance of seeing a difference in experiment outcome; for example, comparing alternative sensors at detection ranges of 1km, 5km, and 10km distances instead of 3km, 5km, and 7km. Increasing the difference between the treatment levels makes it more likely that an experiment will yield larger, more noticeable outcomes.

When the primary action and results during the experiment trial action occur within a simulation, the sensitivity of the simulation to differences between the old and new capabilities should be part of the simulation validation and accreditation effort. New experimental capabilities such as new sensors, new transports, or new weapons that are to be simulated can be rigorously reviewed in simulation prior to the experiment itself. Pre-experiment simulation of the old and new capabilities can also serve to identify simulation conditions that will accentuate outcome differences.

There are two cautions, however, when adjusting scenarios to detect operational differences. First, you might get something you can measure but the scenario may become unrealistic. Secondly, watch out for "experimenter expectancies." This may occur if the scenario is adjusted to obtain a preordained conclusion. In the final analysis, the scenario must be both realistic and sensitive to the discrimination required.

Threat 4. New capability has no opportunity to perform within a trial.

This is the most unfortunate threat in this group. After great effort to counter the first three threats, i.e. getting a fully functional capability on time, providing adequate operator and employment training, and ensuring that the new capability could make a difference, it would be unfortunate if the new capability was never employed during the experiment trials. This can occur when the new capability is not the primary focus of the event, as when conducting embedded experiments within large operational exercises or training exercises, or when conducting a small side-experiment within a larger experiment involving a major operation.

Good practices for preventing Threat 4 include developing a detailed Master Scenario Event List (MSEL) that lists all scenario events that are to occur over the course of the experiment trial. Pre-planned scenario events and scenario injects are specifically developed to drive the experiment players to deal with specific situations that allow for the use of the new capability. The experimenter continually monitors the trial and ensures that the MSEL injects occur. The experimenter should also monitor the experiment players to see if they reacted accordingly to the scenario injects. If the players did not attempt to employ the new capability when the MSEL inject occurred, was it because they did not "see" the scenario inject? For the new capability to succeed or fail on its own merit, it must be employed during the experiment.

SUMMARY

Good practices associated with the above four threats are not new. Paradoxically, they are the most obvious but also the most frequently violated, thereby engendering the most recurring lessons learned in warfighting experiments. Why is this so? The schedule for experiments is fixed in a calendar window because operational forces need long lead times to commit to participation. New capabilities, however, involving innovative software or hardware configurations seldom meet optimistic development schedules. As a result, the experimenter is faced with a dilemma: either execute the experiment during the pre-planned window with the capability functionality "as-is" or forgo the experiment altogether. The operational resources to execute the experiment will lapse at the end of the window whether the experiment is executed or not. Secondly, insufficient time is allocated during the experiment window for player training on the new capability and scenario rehearsals because experiment window durations are minimized to reduce the impact on scarce operational resources. Understanding Threats 1 through 4 and their impact on validity Requirement 1 is the first step toward applying the good practices listed above.

CHAPTER 5

EXPERIMENT REQUIREMENT 2:
ABILITY TO DETECT CHANGE

THE IMPORTANCE OF CHANGE

The basic experiment paradigm is "doing something and seeing what happens." This chapter focuses on the "seeing what happens," or more accurately, "detecting change." Detecting change is reflected in observing or measuring an increase or decrease in the effect variable after each experiment trial. In warfighting experiments, the experimental effect is called the measure of performance (MOP) or measure of effectiveness (MOE). For the discussion in this section, the MOP or MOE will be simply referred to as the "effect."

There is a logical order to the four experiment requirements. If Requirement 1 was not met such that the new capability was either not successfully employed or the scenario was not sensitive to its use, then there is no reason to expect that the new

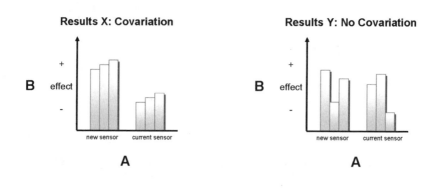

Figure 12. Detecting Change in an Effect

capability would produce a change in the trial outcome. Similarly, we will see that if the experiment did not produce an observable difference in the effect, then it does not make sense to discuss Requirement 3 (the cause of the change) nor to discuss Requirement 4 (the implications of change to a wider context). Therefore, the ability to detect change is the critical second logical requirement.

DETECTING CHANGE
IS OBSERVING COVARIATION

The ability to detect change in the effect is concerned with detecting covariation: a pattern of change between the treatment (A) and the effect (B). Covariation occurs when the size of the effect systematically varies with different applications of the treatment A: the new sensor and the current sensor. A pictorial representation of covariation is presented as Results X in the Figure 12. Results X illustrates a clear pattern between the results of the three trials involving the new sensor and the three trials with the current sensor. On the other hand, if experiment effects (such as targets destroyed, times to detect, amount of supplies delivered) fluctuated widely across the six trials with no discernable pattern corresponding to the two treatments, then no clear covariation will be discernible (Results Y in Figure 12).

Clear covariation represents a high signal-to-noise ratio and presents a discernable pattern between the treatment and effect. A low signal-to-noise ratio presents a difficulty in seeing a pattern of covariation within the experiment noise. The ability to detect trial-to-trial changes is called *statistical validity*. The ability to draw statistical conclusions from an experiment is the ability to detect covariation between different levels of the treatment and the effect. The ability to detect change during an experiment is called *power* in statistics.

MISTAKES IN DETECTING CHANGE

Two different mistakes can be made when deciding whether change was detected or not. The first mistake is *not detecting real change*. Experimenters mistakenly conclude that A and B do not covary when in reality they do. In other words, the experimenter sees Results Y (Figure 12) in the computer printout of the experiment data, but Results X (covariation) is what really occurred in the experiment. In statistics, this error is referred to as a *Type II error*, also known as the producer risk or beta error. Type II error is examined first because most warfighting experiments are "messy." Traditionally, warfighting experiments experience difficulty in detecting change in effectiveness when introducing new capabilities into complex, realistic military operations.

The second mistake is *incorrectly detecting change*. This error occurs when experimenters mistakenly conclude that covaria-

Experiment Component	Threat
Treatment	(5) Capability systems vary in performance.
Player	(6) Experiment players vary in proficiency.
Effect	(7) Data collection accuracy is inconsistent.
Trial	(8) Trial conditions fluctuate.
Analysis	(9) Sample size is insufficient. (10) Statistical assumptions are violated.

Threats 5-9: Failure to detect change (Type II Error)

Threat 10: Incorrect detection of change (Type I Error)

Figure 13. Experiment Requirement 2: Ability to Detect Change

tion exists between the treatment and the effect when in reality it does not. This is akin to seeing covariation (Results X in Figure 12) in the computer printout of the data when Results Y (no covariation) is what really happened. In statistics, this is called a *Type I error*—also known as consumer risk or alpha error. Type I detection error is discussed second since it pertains to technical issues of statistical assumptions and error rates.

The six threats to detecting change can be grouped according to whether they increase the risk of the first or second type of error (Figure 13). The first five threats represent sources of experiment noise that hinder the ability to see real change: Type II threats.

NOT DETECTING REAL CHANGE

Inability to detect real change arises when experimenters incorrectly conclude that a treatment is ineffective. As an example, suppose that in actual military operations a new sensor system would produce quite a few more detections, but the experiment did not produce a discernable increase in effectiveness and the experimenter incorrectly concluded that there was insufficient "goodness" in the new sensor. There was too much noise in the experiment to see the correct signal. The real change was buried in experiment clutter. The ability of experiments to produce discernible results is technically referred to as *statistical power*. The five sources of experiment noise are the five Type II threats to detecting change.

Threat 5. Capability systems vary in performance within a trial.

Performance variability in a new capability increases experiment noise. The first instance occurs when a capability system has to operate continuously over the course of a lengthy trial. Communication systems, sensors, and data systems need to be continuously functioning at a constant level over the course of many hours. Maintaining the consistency of an experimental capability during the entire trial is critical but not always easy in long trials. Prototype systems are often unreliable and may stop functioning during a trial and require unplanned hardware or software modifications during long trials. This random capability variation within a trial diffuses the effectiveness of the treatment and makes it difficult to detect a true change from trial to trial.

Experimenters need to provide sufficient pre-experiment time for immature new technologies to ensure that they will work consistently for the entire duration of a trial. For immature or unreliable systems, experimenters may incorporate an experiment-fix-experiment methodology by designing a series of shorter experiment trials with capability fixes occurring between trials rather than incorporating fixes within long experiment trials. In this manner, the capability is held constant during each trial but allowed to improve from trial to trial in a systematic fashion. This experiment-fix-experiment now has multiple, sequential capability levels that can be examined separately.

Experiment noise also occurs where multiple versions of the capability are employed simultaneously within a single trial; for example, giving all members of a platoon a hand-held radio to see if that improves overall platoon performance. If each hand-held radio functions erratically, any true platoon improvement "signal" may be obscured by the variable performance "noise." Experimenters should calibrate all experiment articles for consistency so that all of the articles are functionally similar within the trial. Experimenters might also use the pilot test to ensure that all copies of the new capability function equivalently. After the experiment, the experimenter can assess the extent of capability variability by comparing individual scores across capability items. When variability is a result of a few discrepant items, the post-experiment analysis can be performed with and without outliers to determine their impact on the results.

Threat 6. Experiment players vary in proficiency within a trial.

Noise from player variability arises in experiments where multiple individuals or multiple teams are used to obtain multiple observations (replications) of one treatment condition, for example, using four different side-by-side gun crews to test the accuracy of a new weapon. Non-standardization among different weapon crews increases error variance. Non-standardization occurs when each of the four crews has a different level of training, a different level of experience, or a different level of motivation.

It is always best to deal with this threat prior to the experiment. Standardization among experiment teams can be improved by training everyone to the same level of performance prior to the start of the trial and selecting similar (homogeneous) players to participate. However, these good practices compromise Requirement 4 (external validity). Actual units are seldom uniform in training and player skills.

After the experiment, the experimenter can assess the extent of standardization by comparing individual scores across player teams. Variability in these scores can sometimes be statistically corrected using covariance analysis with pre-experiment training or experience scores. Post-experiment statistical corrections are always risky due to the statistical assumptions that accompany them. Alternatively, when there are only a few outlier cases, they can be statistically identified and the analysis performed with and without outliers to determine the impact of outliers on the conclusions. However, keep in mind that statistical outliers may, in fact, be real impacts of the future capability and represent a serendipitous finding.

Threat 7. Data collection accuracy is inconsistent within a trial.

Various data collection techniques are available to measure effects in warfighting experiments. Data collection devices include elaborate instrumentation tapping directly into system data busses as well as less elaborate procedures, such as data collectors, questionnaires, and observations from technically proficient raters, referred to as Subject Matter Experts

(SMEs). Inconsistencies in any collection device will obscure true change.

Reliable measurement is the principal good practice for countering variability in data collection. A reliable measure provides consistent output for a particular stimulus. Data collection measures have been divided into two categories: objective and subjective. Objective measures indicate "without human judgment" and include instruments such as laser receivers, in-line counters, cameras, software logger algorithms, and so on. Subjective measures, on the other hand, signify "with human judgment" and include player surveys, data collectors to record visual and acoustical events, and raters to record and infer why an event happened or to evaluate the goodness of an action.

It is incorrect to assume that all objective measures are inherently reliable (consistent) or that all subjective measures are unreliable (inconsistent). All data collection instruments need to be calibrated to ensure their continued consistency throughout the experiment. A good technique is to use objective measures whenever possible. However, they still need to be calibrated. These devices can be calibrated to familiar metrics. For example, a time-stamp recorder may be certified to vary by no more than plus-or-minus two seconds.

Techniques for calibrating the consistency of player surveys and human data collectors are less understood but procedures for doing so do exist.[26] Calibration surveys and data collectors "objectify" traditional subjective measures. Subjective mea-

---

[26] Kass, R.A. "Calibrating questionnaires and evaluators." *The ITEA Journal of Test and Evaluation.* 1984. pp. 3, 26-36.

sures retain human judgment but the human judgment can be made more consistent.

A player questionnaire intended to measure the adequacy or quality of a process or product can be calibrated to quantifiable consistency indices, for example, 0.85 internal-consistency reliability coefficient. Two individuals with similar opinions should result in similar scores on the questionnaire and provide a high consistency index (e.g., 0.85). If they also provided identical response their index would be 1.00. Commercial statistical software programs provide routines (item analysis) that analyze individual questions (items) in surveys to determine their internal consistency with other related items in the survey.

Techniques for increasing survey consistency include increasing the number of related questions about a particular judgment in a questionnaire. Another technique is to avoid eliciting binary responses (yes/no, true/false) when continuous responses are available (for example: 1=never, 2=occasionally, 3=often, 4=always). Binary responses increase variability and limit the efficiency of the statistics that the analyst can employ (discussed below). Using multiple questionnaire items and continuous measures to assess players' responses and calibrating these items using item analysis are good techniques for increasing the objectivity of player surveys.

Similarly, the consistency of data collectors can be calibrated by comparing their observations across similar and dissimilar events during training. The consistency of data-collectors' subjective assessments is enhanced by having individual collectors provide multiple component ratings of a single event (for example, rating both the completeness and usefulness of a report). The component assessments are then combined to produce an overall "adequacy" score.

Additionally, two side-by-side data collectors providing independent assessments can be combined and averaged to provide a more consistent assessment for the trial event. Averaging component scores of a single collector or averaging across multiple collectors increases the reliability of subjective assessments. Training data collectors to provide consistent responses and averaging across data collector responses are good techniques for increasing the consistency of (objectifying) subjective data collector ratings.

Threat 8. Trial conditions fluctuate within a trial.

Uncontrolled variables impacting the effectiveness of the treatment during a trial will artificially increase or decrease the size of the effect for that trial. This unwanted variation will obscure any real differences between trials.

A player unit that experiences different levels of temperature, weather, light conditions, terrain, or threat levels in successive trials will fluctuate in performances during the trial and this noise will obscure any potential effect (signal). While military robustness dictates that useful experimental capabilities be able to stand out under any variation in a military environment, early capabilities may be effective in some, but not all, conditions. If all conditions are allowed to impact randomly, a strong effect in some particular conditions may be obscured in the average.

Early in an experimental program, a good practice is to reduce the number of uncontrolled variables to determine under what conditions an effect can be detected. Additionally, a signal is more likely to be detected in an experiment with a number of shorter trials, each with constant conditions. A signal is less likely to be detected in an experiment with a single long trial that has a wide variety of conditions.

When constant-condition trials are not achievable (or desirable) and the sources of the variability can be identified, some reduction in the variance during the analysis phase can be achieved with experiment designs such as paired comparisons, blocking, and statistical analysis employing analysis of covariance. Each of these statistical techniques can reduce the error term, thus making the signal (treatment effect)-to-noise (error variation) ratio larger and more likely to produce a statistically significant result. However, there is a tradeoff. Each of these techniques also decreases the degrees of freedom associated with the denominator of the error term. These techniques only reduce noise when the reduction in the error variation is not offset by reduction of degrees of freedom. These techniques work best when the matching, blocking, and covariate variables are highly correlated with the effect.

Threat 9. Sample size and overall statistical power is low.

There are three ways to inefficiently employ statistical analysis that jeopardize the ability to observe a real change brought on by employment of the new capability.

Inadequate Sample Size. The larger the sample size is,[27] the more likely it becomes that random variations associated with the

---

[27] See Chapter 10 for an extended discussion of sample size as the number of observations available.

capability, players, data collection, and trial conditions will cancel each other out. Thus, a large sample reduces the impact of noise on detecting the effect. The ability of an experiment to detect an effect of some postulated magnitude is known as the *power* of an experiment. There are available techniques for estimating sample size requirements to achieve specific levels of statistical power. The larger the sample size is, the greater the statistical power will be. It is not true, however, that one must have a sample of 30 or more to obtain statistically significant results. Experiments with as few as 4 or 5 replications can provide statistically significant results provided that one is anticipating large effects (signal) and that experiment variability (noise) from Threats 5, 6, and 7 has been held to a minimum. While sample size is most often the main consideration for determining statistical power, it is not the only contributor.

Setting Type I Risk Too Low. There is a direct correlation between Type I risk (discussed below) and the current Type II risk problem. If the experimenter focuses solely on preventing the Type I error to avoid seeing a result that is due to chance, the experimenter may create conditions that are too stringent, such that a small positive result will not be detected. Accepting more Type I risk (using a risk level of 5 percent rather than 1 percent) increases the statistical power of the analysis technique. Increasing statistical power increases the chance of detecting a small but important difference. When setting the Type I and II risk levels for statistical analysis, experimenters need to consider the consequences of each.

Inefficient Statistical Techniques. Statistical techniques differ in their ability to detect a difference between two sets of numbers. Efficient statistical techniques make finer discriminations and thus have more statistical power. Tests of paired comparisons have more statistical power than tests of independent observations. Parametric techniques are generally more powerful than non-parametric techniques, but require more assumptions about the nature of the data.

INCORRECTLY DETECTING CHANGE

In statistics, a Type I risk is the possibility of incorrectly concluding that A and B covary. This yields the incorrect conclusion that an experiment treatment produced a positive result. If the previous Type II threats are a result of being too conservative, Type I threats can be characterized as being too liberal. Type II mistakes occur more often when the detected difference is small. For example, suppose the average detections for the new sensor was 4.6 while the current sensor was only 4.2. Is this small change an indication of true differences between capabilities? Or is this 9 percent difference due to chance? Of course, the easiest way to *incorrectly* conclude that a small positive result reflects a true difference is to not compute a statistical analysis of the data.

It is a natural tendency to conclude that an experimental system is better after conducting only a few trials (let us say three) and observing a positive result two out of three times. However, we know that flipping a coin three times will yield two heads 38 percent of the time, even though heads and tails are equally likely. Computing statistical analysis of experiment data and getting statistically significant results indicates that the observed positive result did not occur by chance. All experiment results should be subjected to statistical analysis before drawing conclusions about whether the observed change resulted from chance variation or from a difference in treatment capabilities. When conducting statistical analysis, however, the following threat needs to be considered to ensure that the analysis technique itself does not produce the false positive conclusion that it is designed to guard against.

Threat 10. Statistical assumptions are violated and error rate problems occur.

The likelihood of incorrectly detecting a false change increases as the number of statistical comparisons in a single experiment increases. This is relevant when collecting data on many different measures in one experiment, for example, detection times, detection ranges, detection rates, and so on. Binomial probabilities can be used to estimate experiment-wide error. If data for four different measures (k=4) are collected, and each is analyzed in a statistical hypothesis at the 95 percent confidence level (alpha=.05), then there is only a 81 percent confidence $[(1\text{-alpha})^k=(1\text{-.05})^4=.81]$, rather than a 95 percent confidence, that all four hypotheses will be true. In other words, there is a 19 percent probability that at least one of the four individual comparisons is erroneous. A 19 percent chance of an erroneous conclusion is much higher than the advertised 5 percent.

One way to decrease the multiple-comparison error rate is to increase the confidence level for the individual comparisons. One technique is to use a Bonferroni correction. This correction is obtained by dividing the desired alpha level by the number of planned statistical comparisons; in this example 0.05/4=0.0125. A conservative alpha level of 0.0125 instead of 0.05 for each of the four individual comparisons increases the overall confidence level from 81 percent to 95 percent $[(1.0125)^4=.951]$. An alternative to correcting for multiple independent comparisons is to conduct a multivariate analysis of variance (MANOVA).

Every statistical analysis requires certain assumptions about the data. Violating assumptions of statistical tests increases the risk of a Type I error, although sometimes it can also increase the risk of a Type II error. Not all assumptions are equally important. ANOVA is fairly insensitive to departures from assumptions of normality or equal within-cell variances. ANCOVA, on the other hand, is quite sensitive to its requirement for homogeneous within-group regression slopes. Nonparametric techniques require fewer assumptions than parametric statistics concerning the level of measurement and underlying distribution.

During the experiment design stage, evaluating whether the data will meet the assumptions of the planned statistical analysis is based on the experimenters' experience with similar type data. After data collection, most statistical analysis assumptions can be empirically assessed.

INCREASING EXPERIMENT DETECTABILITY

Threats to detecting change arise in all five components of an experiment. Many experimenters focus on sample size as the key. However, Figure 12 indicates that sample size is only a component of low statistical power; and low statistical power is only one of five threats affecting the ability to detect real change. The good news is that experiment detectability is not dependent on sample size alone. All five of the Type II noise threats (Threats 5 through 9) can be ameliorated with good experiment techniques. The key is reducing variability during experiment execution. Attempting to reduce variability after execution by statistical analysis techniques should be the last resort.

There are statistical techniques for estimating the probability of detecting a change of a certain magnitude in a specific effect. This technique is known as *power analysis*. Analysis of statistical power prior to data collection is accomplished by estimating the sample sizes needed for statistical comparisons. After data collection, the experimenter can assess the amount of statistical power that the experiment actually provided.

CHAPTER 6

EXPERIMENT REQUIREMENT 3:

ABILITY TO ISOLATE

THE REASON FOR CHANGE

Once the experimenter has reasonable assurance that the new capability will be employed and that the experiment is designed to detect a change in the effect if it occurs, the next logical question is whether the observed result (B) was caused by the new capability (A) or was a product of some other influence (C). For example, suppose the player unit with the new system was more experienced than the unit with the current system at the start of the experiment. The experimenter could not conclude that an increase in performance for the new system was the result of the new system. The difference may have been a result of the player unit with the new system beginning the experiment with more experience. The ability to identify the correct cause of any observed change is termed *design validity*. Threats to design validity are often referred to as problems of *confounding*.

Confounded results are experiment results that may be attributed to a number of plausible alternate explanations. Confounded results arise when the reason for any observed change in effectiveness cannot be isolated to the intended cause, the new capability. Experiments meeting Requirement 3 validity have eliminated or reduced the potential for alternate explanations for observed changes so that the only remaining explanation is the new capability.

Threats to the ability to isolate the cause of change can be classified into two different groups: threats affecting single group experiments and threats affecting multiple group experiments. A representative single group experiment is displayed in Figure 14. In this example, a single player unit undergoes all four trials employing the current capability and then the new capability in two different scenarios.

In multiple group designs, at least two different player units are involved with a different player unit assigned to the different treatment conditions. Multiple group designs are employed when a second player unit operates an alternative system in a side-by-side comparison experiment. In the example in Figure 14, there are two different units, each with a different capability, and each undergoing two trials. If the alternative capability represents the current baseline system, then the second player unit is called the *control group*.

The single group and multiple group designs have their own sets of validity threats. The single group design will be discussed first.

Single Group Design

	Scenario 1	Scenario 2
Unit C with Current Capability		
Unit C with Future Capability		

One unit receives all treatment conditions.

Multiple Group Design

	Scenario 1	Scenario 2
Unit C with Current Capability		
Unit D with Future Capability		

Different units receive different treatment conditions.

Figure 14. Single versus Multiple Group Design

SINGLE GROUP EXPERIMENT PROBLEMS

The Achilles heel of single group designs is the problem of order effects. Problems arise when attempting to compare early trials to later trials. Trial order distorts comparisons between trial conditions. A simplified pictorial model can illustrate this problem. Figure 15 provides three potential ways to order a sequence of trials: Sequence 1, 2, and 3. To understand the impact of the three sequences, we will imagine that we can quantify what is happening within each separate trial to produce an observable effect. The three numbers below each trial quantify the treatment effect, order effect (learning effect), and observed effect.

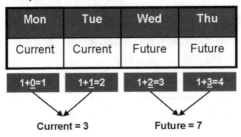

Sequence 1: Unbalanced

Mon	Tue	Wed	Thu
Current	Current	Future	Future
1+0=1	1+1=2	1+2=3	1+3=4

Current = 3   Future = 7

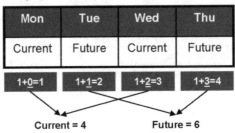

Sequence 2: Balanced

Mon	Tue	Wed	Thu
Current	Future	Current	Future
1+0=1	1+1=2	1+2=3	1+3=4

Current = 4   Future = 6

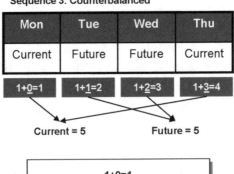

Sequence 3: Counterbalanced

Mon	Tue	Wed	Thu
Current	Future	Future	Current
1+0=1	1+1=2	1+2=3	1+3=4

Current = 5   Future = 5

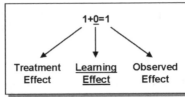

1+0=1

Treatment   Learning   Observed
Effect   Effect   Effect

Figure 15. Sequence Effects in Single Group Designs

Experiment Component	Threat
Treatment	(11) Functionality changes across trials.
Player	(12) Player proficiency changes across trials.
Effect	(13) Data collection accuracy change across trials.
Trial	(14) Trial conditions change across trials.

Figure 16. Single Group Design Threats

The treatment effect is held constant for each trial by giving the treatment effect a quantity of 1 for every trial. A consistent 1 for treatment indicates there is no real difference between the current and future sensors so each had the same effect in their respective trials. Consequently, any observed differences between trials must have resulted from some other factor.

In this simple example, the other factor is the learning effect. In Sequences 1 and 2, the observed increase for the current sensor performance is solely the result of learning. Increases in player task proficiency as a result of experience from one trial to the next are reflected in the increasing numbers: 0, 1, 2, and 3. Sequence 2 indicates that a simple balancing may not be sufficient to counter learning effects. The counterbalanced sequence illustrated in Sequence 3 is the most effective for this example.

Order effects need to be closely monitored in experiments because trials are often sequenced to accommodate resource availability rather than experimental design considerations. For example, electronic countermeasure trials are usually conducted close together (early or late in the sequence) to coincide with the availability and permissibility to use jammers. The four threats listed in Figure 16 occur when a player unit undergoes experiment conditions in some sequence or order.

Threat 11. Capability functionality increases (or decreases) from one trial to the next.

In single group experiments, the functionality of the capability (new system, new process, or new organization) needs to remain constant over time across the different trials in order to assess whether the new capability is equally effective under different trial conditions that occur later in time. If the functionality of the capability increases or decreases over the course of a single group experiment, it will be difficult to disentangle the true cause of any detected change.

Maintaining the consistency of an experimental capability across trials is not always easy. Prototype systems are often unreliable and their performance may decrease during later trials. More likely, however, new systems will undergo modifications during an experiment to correct discovered deficiencies thereby enhancing their functionality in later trials. The key question is whether earlier trials conducted prior to the modification need to be rerun in order to make a comparison to the post-modification trials.

The primary good practice is to allow sufficient time in the pilot test to ensure the stability of the new capability's functionality for the duration of the experiment. During the experiment, the experimenter should continually monitor functionality to ensure that the inherent capability of a treatment does not change during the course of different experiment trials. Monitoring for changes in the treatment, counterbalancing trial sequences when possible, and checking for any increases or decreases in performance over time across successive trials are general good techniques for reducing this threat.

Threat 12. Experiment player proficiency increases (or decreases) from one trial to the next.

Soldiers, airmen, seamen, and marines participating in experiments will change during the event. If the change is one of maturation, players become more experienced and proficient. This is referred to as a *learning effect*. If the change is one of degradation, players become fatigued, bored, or less motivated. Player changes over time will produce an increase or decrease in performance in later trials and this change in performance is unrelated to the change in the designed treatment conditions. This hinders deciphering the real causality of change over sequenced trials.

A good practice is to ensure that player units are trained to maximum performance and operate at a steady state. After the experiment is over, check for increasing or decreasing trends over the temporal sequence of trials.

Since the learning effect dominates warfighting experiments (players become more proficient as the experiment proceeds), the best technique is to counterbalance the sequence as in Sequence 3 of Figure 15. When counterbalancing is not possible, conduct the new capability trial *first* and the current capability trial *last*. The experimenter has deliberately biased the sequence of trials so that learning effects favor the baseline system. Any observed improvement for the new capability when compared to the current capability, has overcome any learning effects. Any performance improvements for the future system can then be credibly attributed to the inherent capability of the new system.

In addition to learning effects, experimenters should monitor player attrition, which might impact trials near the end of an experiment. When possible, compute each trial's outcome for only those players who completed all trials. After the experiment, analyze the trial data arranged by time to determine whether increases or decreases in performance over time occurred irrespective of the nature of the trial. If temporal increases or decreases are found, analysis of covariance can be used (with caution) to statistically correct for unrelated temporal changes.

Threat 13. Data collection accuracy increases (or decreases) from one trial to the next.

There is always a danger that observed effects may be due to changes in the data collection instrumentation or procedures rather than changes in the test unit performance. As the experiment progresses, data collectors gain experience and change their opinions as to what constitutes effective or ineffective responses; or they may become careless and less observant. Similarly, data collection instrumentation may change for the better or worse. Instrumentation technicians may improve their procedures, making them more precise. Conversely, instruments may deteriorate if they lose calibration.

These threats are reduced by monitoring for changes in the data collection procedures, counterbalancing the trial sequence when possible, monitoring for any increases or decreases in collection performance over time, and re-calibrating sensitive data collection instrumentation before the start of each trial. Also, experimenters should monitor for data collector attrition or data collector substitution after the experiment has started. When possible, compute each trial's outcome for those data collectors who completed all trials to see if their responses differ from those who did not complete all trials.

When the experiment is completed, analyze the trial data by time to determine whether performance increases or decreases irrespective of the nature of the trial. If temporal increases or decreases are found, analysis of covariance can be used to statistically correct for unrelated temporal changes.

Threat 14. Trial conditions become easier (or more difficult) from one trial to the next.

This threat represents all of the uncontrolled variables found in the experiment setting such as weather, terrain, light conditions, starting conditions, and free-play tactics. To the extent these variables fluctuate randomly throughout the experiment, they constitute Threat 8 to the possibility of detecting change, Requirement 2. However, to the extent that they change non-randomly and produce an overall increase or decrease in performance over the sequence of trials, they constitute a threat to Requirement 3 by providing alternative causes of change in performance from trial to trial.

Good practices include exerting control over the trial execution conditions, monitoring any changes in the test setting from trial to trial, counterbalancing trial sequence when possible, and checking for any increases or decreases in performance over time across trials. In experiments with a large number of trials, one could randomize the sequence of the trials. This situation seldom occurs, however. With fewer experiment trials, it is always best to order them manually in a manner that will best mitigate any sequence effects.

MULTIPLE GROUP EXPERIMENT PROBLEMS

The sequence of trials is no longer a primary concern in multiple group designs. If both the future system player unit and the control unit conduct their Scenario 1 trials first and Scenario 2 trials last (see Figure 17), any artificial increase or decrease in the subsequent Scenario 2 trials will affect both groups equally. Comparisons between the two groups for performance differences during Scenario 2 trials are immune to order effect threats as long as both groups undergo trials in the same sequence, the rate of change for both groups is similar, and the focus of the analytic comparison is *between groups* rather than *within groups*. That is, we are more interested in comparing the future system to the current system Scenario 2 trials (*between group* comparison) rather than comparing the future system in Scenario 1 to its performance in Scenario 2 (*within group* comparison).

The primary concern in multiple group designs is the potential for confounding due to the association of separate treatments with different player groups. Figure 18 depicts the three threats to isolating the true cause of change for *between group* comparisons. Notice there is no threat associated with the treatment component. The purpose of the multiple group design is to create differences between groups based on giving different treatments (or different levels of a treatment) to the different groups. The critical concern for validity is to ensure that this treatment difference between groups is the only difference between the groups by carefully managing the other three experiment components.

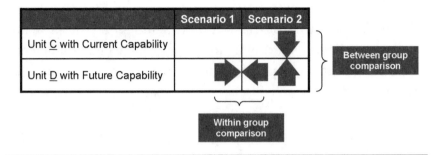

Figure 17. Multiple Group Design

Experiment Component	Threat
Player	(15) Groups differ in player proficiency.
Effect	(16) Data collection accuracy differs for each group.
Trial	(17) Groups operate under different trial conditions.

Figure 18. Multiple Group Design Threats

Threat 15. Experiment groups differ in player proficiency.

Inherent differences between player units may result in spurious differences between treatment groups. Assignment of different units to different conditions is necessary when a player unit cannot undergo both treatment conditions sequentially, when a single player unit cannot be expected to operate both the old and new system in succession. When different player units undergo different treatment conditions, there is always the danger that the results will reflect differences between the units, rather than differences created by the treatment systems. There are six group characteristics to be considered.

Threat 15-1. Initial Group Differences.

This is the major consideration. Player units may differ at the beginning of the experiment in a way that will influence the outcome. Initial group differences arise because of unequal group assignment.

- Random assignment to the different experiment groups is the best technique. In an experiment involving a large number of players, let us say 50 riflemen, it is possible to randomly assign the soldiers to different treatment conditions, for example, current weapon and future weapon. The advantage of randomization is that it equates the two groups on all characteristics (measurable and non-measurable) that could affect the experiment results. Unfortunately, randomization only works when a large number of experimental units (individual soldiers, teams, crews, and sections) are in the experiment and random assignment does not affect unit integrity.

- In small groups, equality between groups is improved by guided assignment of individuals to groups rather than random assignment. Random assignment does not work well with small heterogeneous groups. For example, if an experiment involving physical exercises required 6 individuals in two treatment groups and the pool of 12 subjects consisted of 6 males and 6 females, then pure random assignment would probably yield an unequal number of males and females in each of the two treatment groups. In this instance, a "stratified" random assignment would be better. That is, randomly assign 3 of the males and 3 of the females to each group. Even better in small experiments is to match individuals on critical traits and then randomly assign one of each pair to a treatment group. To achieve equal assignment in experiments, experimenters should measure all characteristics of the player units that affect experiment outcome: e.g. years of experience, gender, and rank. Assignment to treatment conditions based on these measured traits is an attempt to make the player groups equal at the start of the experiment. However, assigning matched individuals to different treatment groups is seldom possible because soldiers come to the experiment as part of an existing unit and most warfighting experiments involve integral player units. Assignment based on measured traits, even when feasible, is probably not very effective. Those traits most likely to influence the outcome—motivation and leadership—are hardest to measure.

- When it is not feasible to equate treatment groups before the experiment, inherent group differences can be ameliorated by experiment design manipulations. One technique is to have each group participate as its own baseline. An example is a field evaluation of two competing advanced helicopters X and Y. Six pilots who flew advanced helicopter X also flew the current baseline helicopter. Six additional pilots who flew advanced helicopter Y also flew the current baseline helicopter. The results showed that version X performed better than version Y. However, when the two groups of pilots were compared head-to-head in the baseline helicopter, the version X pilots also performed better than the version Y pilots. Thus, the correct interpretation is that no performance differences attributable to helicopter differences were found. Performance differences were correctly attributed to initial, inherent group differences.

Threat 15-2. Evolving Group Differences.

Treatment groups assessed as equivalent at the start of an experiment may not be equivalent at the experiment's end. This occurs in long experiments that continue for several weeks or months and players in the different treatment conditions drop out at different rates. Dropouts, or "experiment casualties," are individuals who leave before completion of the experiment for any number of reasons, such as emergency leave or change of assignment. Artificial group differences may evolve when more players in one experimental condition drop out than in the second condition. A differential dropout rate does not result in initial group differences. Instead, it results in differences between groups after the experiment has started even though the groups may have been equivalent at the beginning of the experiment. A good practice is to monitor experiment casualties in long experiments for their potential impact on group results.

Threat 15-3. Designed Group Differences.

Some experiments are designed to begin with non-equivalent groups. In experiments of training devices, operators who scored low on some index are assigned additional training on an experimental new training system. For example, operators with low marksmanship scores may be assigned to an experimental laser rifle training program. The danger in assigning individuals to treatment groups based on prior performance is that their performance will improve automatically. Individuals with low pre-experiment scores will exhibit higher post-experiment scores while individuals with high pre-experiment scores will exhibit lower post-experiment scores. This shift towards the middle of the score range (regression towards the mean) occurs in the absence of any additional training and is a result of the measurement error in the pre-experiment testing. Consequently, players assigned to a training condition based on low scores will show an improvement even if the new training system is irrelevant to performance.

To reduce this risk, establish a control group. Operators with low pre-experiment scores would be assigned randomly to two groups: a control group and the new training group. The control group would not participate in any remedial training. While both groups will show improvement upon retesting, if the new training group shows more improvement than the control group, a case can be made for the utility of the new training system.

Threat 15-4. Unintentional Designed Group Differences.

Group differences can unintentionally occur before the formal experiment begins; for example, if only one of two equivalent player units is required to undergo pre-experiment activities. If Unit X is required at the experiment site two weeks early for extra training with practice scenarios to develop techniques for employing the new capability, then Unit X will approach the experiment differently than Unit Y.

Threat 15-5. Group Dominator Differences.

When treatment groups are small (one crew or one team), one individual may drastically influence the group score for better or for worse. Larger groups are the best remedies. When this is not possible, analysts should examine data for group dominator effects, sometimes referred to as outliers. Group results can be analyzed with and without outliers included to see if con-clusions are reversed.

Threat 15-6. Group Motivation Differences.

When multiple groups participate in an experiment, each group knows they are being compared to another group. Group identity engenders *esprit de corps* within a group and competitiveness between groups. While participant motivation to perform well in the experiment is critical, a threat to validity occurs when the separate treatment groups are operating under different motivations; thereby confounding the interpre-tation of any treatment differences. There are three variations of this theme.

- **Imitation.** One group may imitate another group rather than respond to its own treatment. For example, in an experiment in which manual and automated intelli-gence analysis systems are compared, the two groups may share information during lunch breaks. Conse-quently, the group using the manual process may imitate the responses of the group using the automated process. Not only does this exchange of information diffuse any potential performance difference between two groups, the group using the manual procedure no longer reflects an operational unit using only manual procedures. A good practice is to keep competing groups separate throughout the experiment.

- **Compensation.** This is called the "John Henry" effect." When individuals are aware that they are being evaluated in a less desirable or more strenuous condi-tion, they may push harder to outperform those in the easier condition. Experiment players in a baseline condition may strive harder to demonstrate that they are better than the unit selected (with the accompanying publicity) to receive the new, potentially superior system. Experimentation results would run counter to the hypotheses and would be a result of motivation rather than the intended treatment.

- **Resentment.** This is the opposite of compensation. Experiment players in the less desirable experimental condition may perform poorly as a result of being selected for this condition rather than the more desirable condition. Their poor performance would exaggerate any actual effect due to the experimental conditions.

Good techniques for compensation and resentment are not always easy to find. At minimum, the experimenter needs to continually monitor the attitudes and motivations of different groups so that the impact of these threats can be considered if they occur. Providing equivalent publicity and recognition to all groups in the experiment will help to offset the natural feelings for compensation and resentment.

Threat 16. Data collection accuracy differs among the experiment groups.

The same amount of effort to ensure that two different player units are equal should be invested to ensure that data collection methods for each treatment group are equal. In side-by-side comparison experiments, different data collectors are often assigned to the different experiment player units. Are the data collectors assigned to different groups really equivalent? Data collectors and the accuracy and reliability of the instrumentation for each group need to be equal. Additionally, the allocation of data collection devices between different experiment groups may reflect the experimenter's expectations. Rosenthal[28] has described how the "experimenter's expectancies" concerning the outcome of an experiment may bias the data obtained (and even the subsequent data analysis). Expectations concerning which evaluated system should be better may bias the results if data is collected differently. When this occurs, it is difficult to know whether the reported outcome is a result of the intended treatment or a result of the differences in data collection procedures.

A good practice is to ensure that the new capability group does not get all of the best instrumentation and most proficient data collectors. The experimentation team and the analysts must continually scrutinize their own motivation to ensure that their "expectancies" are not biasing the data collection and analysis.

The *double-blind* experiment technique is used extensively in medical research to guard against experimenter expectancies and group motivational differences (Threat 15-6). In double-blind experiments, neither the administrator of the treatment nor the patient knows which treatment group they are aligned with. Double-blind techniques are difficult to implement in warfighting experiments because it is usually obvious to everyone when a new capability is being employed.

---

[28] Rosenthal, R. *Experimenter Effects in Behavioral Research*. New York: Appleton-Century-Croft. 1966.

Threat 17. Experiment groups operate under different trial conditions.

This threat represents the uncontrolled variables found in the experimental setting such as weather, terrain, tactics, and opposing forces (OPFOR) experience (Red players). To the extent that uncontrolled trial variables impact the different experiment groups differently, these influences constitute a threat to Requirement 3 by making it difficult to interpret differences in group performance.

This threat is always present in field experiments because two different player units cannot occupy the same terrain and execute the same trial at the same time. There will always be some trial differences. The goal is to minimize any difference that may affect the outcome of the trial. The best practice to minimize this threat is to execute as much of the trial as possible simultaneously for each treatment group. Experiments on detection systems allow the simultaneous presentation of targets to all experiment groups. This ensures that all environmental and most target characteristics are the same for all sensors. To ensure equality of the target aspect angle, a sensor's position can be alternated after each trial. Monitoring any differences in the experimental setting between groups and counterbalancing the trial sequence between groups when possible also reduces this threat.

SUMMARY

Assessment of Requirement 3 (the ability to isolate the reason for change) is a logical assessment. This is in contrast to Requirement 2 (the ability to detect change), which can be evaluated statistically. The assessment of Requirement 3 requires knowledge of what factors other than the new capability might affect the experiment results. Careful consideration and monitoring of the ongoing experiment can neutralize many of the threats. Attention to Requirement 3 will allow experimenters to interpret results in a clear, unambiguous manner, attributing any changes in the outcome to the new capability alone. Chapter 9 provides additional discussion of arranging the sequence and number of trials to offset these threats.

CHAPTER 7

EXPERIMENT REQUIREMENT 4:
ABILITY TO RELATE RESULTS
TO ACTUAL OPERATIONS

Let us now suppose that the experimenter was successful in employing the new capability, detecting change, and isolating the cause. The question is now whether the experimental results are applicable to operational forces in actual military operations. The ability to relate results from the experiment setting to the operations of interest is termed *operational validity*. This fourth experiment requirement is the easiest to understand but the most difficult to achieve. It is easy to understand that a warfighting experiment ought to represent actual military operations. It is difficult to achieve because many operational conditions of importance are difficult to represent in the experiment environment. The more operational conditions represented in the experiment, the easier it is to

Experiment Component	Threat
Treatment	(18) Functionality does not represent future capability.
Player	(19) Players do not represent operational unit.
Effect	(20) Measures do not reflect important effects.
Trial	(21) Scenario is not realistic.

Figure 19. Threats to the Ability to Relate Results

provide evidence that experiment results will be applicable to an operational unit in an operational situation.

THREATS THAT DIMINISH EXPERIMENT GENERALIZABILITY

Experiment results are only useful to the extent that they say something about the real world. *Generalizability* is the scientific term for the ability to apply results outside the experiment context. The ability to relate results pertains to experiment realism. The four threats listed in Figure 19 limit the realism of the experiment, making it more difficult to translate results from the experiment to real-world military operations.

Threat 18. Experiment surrogate functionality does not represent potential future capability.

Future systems in warfighting experiments are rarely suffi- ciently mature to give confidence in their embodiment of future functionality. First, new capabilities continually evolve during and after the experiment. As the capability evolves post-experiment, it will be difficult to match the experiment results to evolving functionality. More importantly, new capa- bilities are dependent on surrogates during experimentation

and the question is to what extent does the surrogate sufficiently represent the future "real" capability in order to
conclude that the experiment findings are relevant to the use
of this future capability?

Very early idealized surrogates tend to be overly optimistic in
representing future capability. These optimistic surrogates are
useful, however, in examining the worth of pursuing a particular capability further. These experiments investigate whether
an optimized capability can markedly improve warfighting
effectiveness. If the experiment results are negative, there may
be sufficient reason not to explore further because even the
optimistic solution did not solve the problem. On the other
hand, positive results make a case for further experimentation
on more realistic surrogates to get a more accurate estimate of
potential effect.

Interestingly, as subsequent surrogates become more realistic,
sometimes referred to as prototypes, they tend to underesti-
mate the potential future capability. As the surrogates
incorporate more of the software and hardware of the final
configuration, there are inevitable functionality deficiencies
brought on by immaturity of the prototype. The interpretation
of experiments with "under-representative surrogates" that
produce low effects is much more difficult. Were the low effects
due to the poor representation of the prototype such that a
more functional prototype would have yielded better results?
In this situation, capability proponents will always be accused
of wishful thinking. As surrogates approach the realism of prototypes, more time is required prior to the experiment to
ensure that it has sufficient and stable functionality or the
experiment will not be interpretable.

A good practice is to accurately report the strengths and limitations of the surrogates and prototypes used in the experiment. When experiments are used as the final assessment to decide whether a new capability should be deployed to the operating forces, it is critical to use fully functional prototypes for accurate estimates of effectiveness. On the other hand, use of surrogates with major limitations is permitted, even encouraged, in early experimentation in the concept development cycle. These early surrogates permit a preliminary look at the system's potential military utility and identify early human-factors requirements. Early experiments with surrogates and prototypes also provide influence design decisions. However, the limited ability to relate conclusions from prototypes to production systems needs to be recognized.

Threat 19. Experiment players do not represent intended operational unit.

How well do the experiment players represent operators and operational units that will eventually employ the experimental capability? There are three related issues in this threat: (1) the prior experience of the experiment players, (2) their level of training on the new capability, and (3) their motivation for participating in the experiment.

A good technique is to select experiment players directly from an operational unit that will eventually employ the capability. Often, however, experiments use reservists, retired military, or government civilians due to the unavailability of operational forces. This is not a major threat when the task represents basic human perception or cognition. However, if the experiment represents a military task under combat conditions, the absence of actual experienced military personnel jeopardizes the applicability of any observed effects.

Even when operational forces are available, the experimenter has to be concerned about the appropriate level of training on the new capability. If the experiment unit is under-trained or over-trained, the true capabilities of soldiers in a typical unit will be misrepresented. Under-training results from compressed schedules to start the experiment and inadequate training procedures for new concepts or new systems. Over-training arises when player units undergo unique training not planned for units that will receive the fielded systems. Over-training, like under-training, is difficult to avoid.

Always ensure that the experiment unit is well-qualified to operate the experimental systems and experimental concept so that the systems and concept will be given a fair evaluation. The temptation is to over-train the experiment unit to ensure success. An over-trained experiment unit is referred to as a "golden crew." The challenge is to produce a well-trained, typical unit rather than an over- or under-trained unique experiment unit.

Player motivation is always a concern in experiments. Since motivation effects performance, the concern is the extent to which the participant's motivation represents the same motivation expected in the actual environment. In the actual environment, it is expected that military personnel will work extremely hard to achieve their mission under any condition. In the experiment, this same motivation needs to occur and most often it does because participants are professionals and want to excel. Constructing a realistic experiment setting, discussed later in Threat 21, is also important to enhancing player motivation.

Three specific concerns can influence player motivation to unrealistically under- or over-perform during an experiment. When personnel are assigned to participate in the experiment as an "additional" duty and it is perceived to be unrelated to their real mission, participants may under-perform out of resentment or lack of interest.

On the other hand, players may over-perform due to being in the experiment spotlight. This is known as the "Hawthorne effect," when it was found that factory workers increased productivity, not because of different experimental illumination levels in the workplace, but because the workers were being observed. The Hawthorne effect is more likely to occur in highly visible experiments with high-ranking visitors. In this instance, the players are motivated to make the capability "look good" to please the audience even though the capabilities may not be that effective. That experiment players are motivated to do well in the experiment reflects motivated warfighters in the operational environment. When the experiment players attempt to excel by "gaming" the experiment however, the relevance of the experiment is lowered.

A third concern is the possibility of inducing "player expectancies," where players perform according to the expectancies of the experimenter (also known as the Pygmalion effect). If the experimenter expects the control group to do poorer than the new capability group, the control group may perceive this and perform accordingly.

Experimenters must continually monitor the motivation of the participants. Sufficient time has to be allocated to explain the importance of the experiment and their contribution to the effort, emphasizing that the success of the experiment is not whether the capability produces a positive result but that it was thoroughly and realistically employed so that it can be honestly evaluated.

Threat 20. Experiment measures do not reflect important warfighting effects.

Ensuring representative measures is easier when examining the effects of new capabilities on relatively simple military outcomes such as targets detected, targets destroyed, transit time, and so on. For these outcomes, the primary concern is measurement bias. A biased data collection device would over- or under-represent the effect of the new capability. Thus the effectiveness of the capability in the experiment would not represent its future potential, for better or worse. Measurement precision,[29] in this context, means that the output is unbiased. It does not measure to the left or right of the true value. A technique for ensuring the precision of simple measures is calibrating the data collection instrumentation to ensure its accuracy prior to the experiment.

Non-biased measures are more difficult to achieve when the new capability is attempting to achieve a complex result, such as information superiority, improved planning, better decisions, increased situational awareness, better collaboration, or mis-

---

[29] Measurement precision has two elements: non-biased and consistent. Threat 20 emphasizes the non-biased aspect, avoiding either under- or over-estimates. The reader may recall that the earlier discussion under Threat 7 emphasized the consistency aspect—estimates with small variability. Both consistency and non-bias are essential to measurement precision. Consistency applies to Experiment Requirement 2 (ability to detect a result). Non-bias applies to Requirement 4 (ability to relate the results). Detecting a "consistent signal" that is offset (biased) from the actual signal is a threat to validity, an inability to translate experiment estimates of results to the operational environment.

sion success. These complex operational concepts are difficult to define and, not surprisingly, are difficult to measure in actual operations and in warfighting experiments. There are two general techniques to develop non-biased measures of complex outcomes. Each has its own strengths and weaknesses.

Combine concrete components of complex effects. Overall unit effectiveness, for example, may be definable in terms of concrete, discrete, measurable variables such as loss-exchange ratio, rate of movement, and time to complete a mission. Individual component scores can be combined into a weighted (or unweighted) composite score to represent the complex effect. There are several problems with this approach.

Component measures may not covary in a similar fashion. In some instances, a slow rate of movement may be associated with a low loss ratio. In other instances, it could be associated with a high loss ratio. While the individual component variable scores can be reported, these scores by themselves do not address the overall unit effectiveness that is the measure of interest. An alternative approach is to select a single component measure that represents the highest level of interest in the complex variable.

A second problem is the "halo effect." When measuring multiple components of a complex variable, analysts need to ensure that the individual components are measured independently of each other. If all of the components are measured in the same manner, any covariation among the component indices cannot be disassociated from the influence of its measurement method. This is especially problematic when the sole data source for all component measures is an expert rater or questionnaire. For example, if a single rater provides estimates for a unit's ability to maneuver, to collect intelligence, and to engage the enemy, and these three estimates are combined into a unit effectiveness score, then the covariation of these component measures may be artificially high due to a halo effect. Any inaccuracy in the single data source (a single rater) induces the same bias error in each component score resulting in an inflated component covariation. A technique to avoid this halo effect is to collect component data using independent sources (raters, participant surveys, instrumentation) whenever possible.

Measure Complex Effects with an Overall Subjective Rating. An expert rater can provide an overall assessment rating for the complex variable of interest. This alleviates the problem of defining, measuring, and combining data from component measures. However, the use of subjective ratings brings its own set of problems: potential inconsistency and bias. A biased judgment is one that is "consistently off the mark" whereas an inconsistent judgment is one that is "sometimes on and sometimes off the mark." The problem of inconsistency was discussed previously under Threat 7. The problem of bias will be discussed here.

A good technique for calibrating bias in subjective ratings is to continually assess inter-rater agreement of raters observing the same event. Secondly, it is important for them to observe predetermined "good" and "poor" practice events in training to determine if their assessments vary correspondingly. During the experiment execution, it is important to collect objective quantitative component scores in addition to the subjective composite ratings. Confidence increases in subjective ratings to the extent that they correlate to the independently obtained objective component measures. Another way to increase the "objectivity" of "subjective" ratings is to employ several raters independently[30] and combine their individual scores into a single overall assessment. And finally, the veracity of ratings rest on the operational experience and credibility of the raters.

Threat 21. Experiment scenario is not realistic.

How realistic is the experiment scenario for the Blue and Red force participants? While this is the twenty-first threat, it is not the least of the threats. The threat numbering system does not denote priority. Scenario realism is often viewed as the most critical element in military exercises and, similarly, in warfighting experiments. Scenarios that do not meet sufficient realism may invalidate the entire experiment from this perspective.

Realistic Blue Force Operations. Many factors make it difficult for the experimental unit to use realistic tactics, techniques, and procedures. Modifying current Blue force tactics to incorporate new capabilities often follows, rather than precedes, new capability development. Even when new techniques and procedures have been developed, adequate training is difficult due to surrogate shortages until experiment execution. Additionally, terrain, instrumentation, or safety restraints during experiment execution may preclude appropriate tactical maneuvering during field experiments.

---

[30] The prior discussion for combining independent rating is thoroughly discussed under Threat 7. For Threat 7, the intent was to reduce variability. Here, the intent is to reduce bias. The techniques discussed under Threat 7 accomplish both goals. One of the reviewers of this manuscript reminded me that combining independent assessments into an average estimate has been shown to be superior to estimates provided by individual experts. For multiple examples of this in economics and business, see: Surowiecki, James. *The Wisdom of Crowds.* New York, NY: Anchor Press. 2005.

Good practices include allocating sufficient time for training the experiment unit in appropriate tactics with the new capability. Tactical units can assist the experimenter in developing realistic operational plans that provide for appropriate force ratios, missions, and maneuver space and time.

Realistic Setting. There are two aspects to ensuring a realistic environment in which to examine the new capability. The first aspect concerns the ability of the experiment setting to sufficiently represent the operational envelope of the new capability. Examining the complete operational envelope might entail having sufficient and appropriate targets available, appropriate engagement ranges, different day and night conditions, different supporting elements, and so on. Good practices include identifying the critical aspects of the capabilities' operational envelope, those to be included in the experiment and those that will not be included due to resource constraints or other reasons. This latter group is listed as experiment limitations. When particular operational envelope elements are believed to be critical to the success or failure of the new capability, these should be systematically varied in different trials so the impact of each can be measured separately.

The second aspect of a realistic setting is the ability to create conditions during an experiment that approximate the noise, confusion, fear, and uncertainty of combat. Increasing the realism of player participation is a good practice for offsetting the potential lack of player apprehension during field trials. The use of lasers to simulate engagements increases the realism of tactical engagements. Other techniques include running the experiment trial for many hours or days to generate fatigue-associated stress.

Over time, experiment players can anticipate and prepare for scenario events. Directing a unit to an assembly area during continuous operations to calibrate instrumentation is a signal to the unit that a battle will soon occur. Surprise has evaporated. Additionally, player units that undergo the same scenario over successive trials know what to expect. Anticipation of scenario events decreases apprehension and promotes non-representativeness of unit reactions. Good practices allow for maximum free play and sufficient scenario space to promote player uncertainty, player creativity, and sufficient opportunity to explore and attempt to solve the warfighting problem.

Realistic Reactive Threat. Representation of threat tactics and equipment in the experiment is a special difficulty. Captured threat equipment is not always available for field experiments and training operational units to emulate threat tactics is a low priority except at centralized training centers. It is difficult to imagine what the adversary would do in any given situation. It is all too easy to imagine and rationalize what the United States would do in a similar situation. History has shown, however, that irrational leaders do exist and we should not always prepare for the rational, mirror-image adversary.

Conducting field experiments at the national training centers, when possible, enhances realism because they can provide realistic, well-trained threats. When not conducting experiments in the field, use threat experts from the national agencies to assist in designing the threat in the experiment scenarios and to monitor the conduct of the threat during execution. During trial execution, the threat should be given maximum free play to respond to and even preempt, if possible, Blue force employment of the new experimental capability.

The development and employment of an intelligent, determined opposing force is one of the best counters to the threat of non-representative scenarios.

SUMMARY

Experiments can never be perfect representations of actual combat operations. Meeting Requirement 4 depends on approximating the operational conditions to which the conclusions of the experiment are pertinent. All experiments are approximations to operational realism. The assessment of operational validity rests on judgments as to the representativeness of the system, the measures, the player unit, the scenario, and the site conditions under which the experiment was conducted.

Many of the practices for validating experiment realism are similar to the techniques used in the validation of models and simulation (M&S), especially the idea of "face validity." In most cases, experts inside and outside the Department of Defense are employed to certify or validate the prototype's capabilities, the scenario, the threat, and the operations in the experiment or simulation. Where possible, some "predictive validity" techniques may be employed to the extent that conditions in the experiment scenario can be related to real-world exercises, deployments, and operational lessons learned.

CHAPTER 8

IMPROVING INDIVIDUAL EXPERIMENTS

The preceding chapters provide the detailed enumeration of experiment techniques organized within the experiment logic explicated in Chapter 4. The real power of the logic, however, is its guide to experimenters in evaluating the strengths and weaknesses of different types of warfighting experiments. All experiments have strengths and weaknesses. There is no such thing as a perfect experiment. This is true whether the experiment is conducted in a laboratory or in the field.

Knowing the strengths and weaknesses of particular experiments *in advance* of experiment execution allows the experimenter to decide which strengths should be emphasized for a particular experiment. To do this, experimenters need to understand why the experiment is being conducted, who it is conducted for, and the consequences of experiment success or failure. Cognizance of the strengths and limitations of the impending experiment allows experimenters to more realistically apprise the experiment stakeholders (those with an interest in the experiment outcome) of what the experiment will return for their investment. Experiments can provide a wealth of empirical support for transformation decisions, but no single experiment can do it all.

NO PERFECT EXPERIMENT

Internal Validity

Requirement 1: Ability to Use the New Capability
Requirement 2: Ability to Detect Change
Requirement 3: Ability to Isolate the Reason for Change

External Validity

Requirement 4: Ability to Relate Results to Actual Operations

A fundamental fall-out from these four experiment requirements is that a 100 percent valid experiment is not achievable. The four experiment requirements cannot be fully satisfied in one experiment. Satisfying one works against satisfying the other three. Thus, decisions need to be made as to which validity requirements are to be emphasized in any given experiment.

All experiments are a balance between internal and external validity requirements. The first three requirements represent the internal validity of the experiment, the ability to determine if a causal relationship exists between two variables. The fourth represents external validity, the ability to generalize the cause-and-effect relationship found in the experiment environment to the operational military environment.

Precision and control increase internal validity (ability to detect and isolate change) but often lead to decreases in external validity (ability to relate results to actual operations). Experiments that emphasize free play and uncertainty in scenarios represent conditions found in real operations and satisfy Requirement 4, the ability to relate results. Conversely, experiments emphasizing control of trial conditions and sample size satisfy the internal validity Requirements 2 and 3, the ability to detect and isolate change.

The idea that there are no perfectly valid experiments along with the long list of experiment techniques presented in Chapters 4 through 7 make it appear as though warfighting experimentation is too hard. Shadish, Cook, and Campbell (2003) write that experimenters need not be skeptics but rather cognizant experimenters:

> This [long list of validity threats] might lead readers to wonder if any single experiment can successfully avoid all of them. The answer is no. We can not reasonably expect one study to deal with all of them simultaneously, primarily because of logical and practical tradeoffs among them that we describe in this section. Rather, the threats to validity are heuristic devices that are intended to raise consciousness about priorities and tradeoffs, not to be a source of skepticism or despair. Some are more important than others in terms of prevalence consequences for quality of inference, and experience helps the researcher to identify those that are more prevalent and important for any given context. It is more realistic to expect a program of research to deal with most or all of these threats over time. Knowledge growth is more cumulative than episodic, both with experiments and with any type of research. However, we do not mean all

this to say that single experiments are useless or all
equally full of uncertainty in the results. A good
experiment does not deal with all threats, but only
with a subset of threats that a particular field considers most serious at the time.[31]

Validity priorities can differ for any given experiment. Experimenters need to minimize the loss of one validity requirement
because of the priority of another. However, tradeoff is inevitable. In settings where one expects a small effect and it is
important to determine the precise relationship between the
experiment treatment and its effect, the priority should be
internal validity. On the other hand, if one expects a large
effect and it is important to determine if the effect will occur in
the operational environment with typical units, then external
validity is the priority.

THE IMPORTANCE OF REQUIREMENT 3: THE ABILITY TO ISOLATE THE REASON FOR CHANGE

In most warfighting experiments, indeed in most experiments
of any kind, a case can be made for special consideration to
satisfying Requirement 3. The ability to isolate the reason for
change can be considered the *sine qua non* of conducting an
experiment. Resolving cause and effect is essential to interpreting the experiment results. If one cannot ascribe the observed
change to some cause with some degree of certainty, the experiment is uninterpretable.[32]

---

[31] Shadish et al., *Experimental and Quasi-Experimental Designs.* p. 96.
[32] Ibid., p. 99.

That is, to do an experiment and have no interest in internal validity [cause and effect] is an oxymoron. Doing an experiment makes sense only if the researcher has an interest in a descriptive causal question, and to have this interest without a concomitant interest in the validity of the causal answer seems hard to justify.[33]

Internal validity, especially in Requirements 1, 2, and 3, is critical to all warfighting experiments. A very realistic field experiment may be conducted, but in the end, if the experimenter cannot make a case for or against the new capability with some degree of assurance, then the experiment can turn out to be an expensive training exercise for the player units. A case for a capability can be made when something different happens in an experiment and this difference can be attributed solely to the introduction of the new capability.

To ensure a sufficient level of validity to meet Requirement 3, some operational realism may need to be sacrificed. In an evaluation of a new gas mask for tank crews, for example, a data collector may replace one of the crewmembers, such as a loader. While this detracts from crew integrity, it provides data for evaluating mask effectiveness during operations. Similarly, a scenario calling for continuous operations may have to be interrupted periodically to collect data from the participants. In a final example, to ensure that two player units are at similar levels of proficiency in a multiple group design experiment, one unit may require more training to equal the other unit, even though all units are not equal in the operational forces.

---

[33] Shadish et al., *Experimental and Quasi-Experimental Designs.* p. 99.

The Importance of Requirement 3: The Ability to Isolate the Reason for Change

Requirement 3, the ability to isolate the reason for change, is most often the critical reason for conducting experiments. This is not to say that the other requirements never rise in importance; the next two sections will show that they do. Every effort should be made to minimize the impact of increasing one requirement over any of the other three.

DIFFERENT WARFIGHTING EXPERIMENTATION METHODS PROVIDE DIFFERENT STRENGTHS

Most warfighting experiments can be grouped into one of four general methods (Figure 20): *analytic wargame, constructive, human-in-the-loop,* and *field experiments.* Each of the four methods has its own strengths and weaknesses with respect to the four experiment requirements discussed above. Since one particular experiment method cannot satisfy all four requirements, a comprehensive experiment campaign requires multiple experiment methods.

Analytic wargame experiments typically employ command and staff officers to plan and execute a military operation. At certain decision points, the Blue players give their course of action to a neutral, White Cell, which then allows the Red players to plan a counter move, and so on. The White Cell adjudicates each move, using a simulation to help determine the outcome. A typical wargame experiment might involve fighting the same campaign twice, using different capabilities each time. The strength of wargame experiments resides in the ability to detect any change in the outcome, given major differences in the strategies used. Additionally, to the extent that operational scenarios are used and actual military units are players, wargame experiments may reflect real-world possibilities. A major

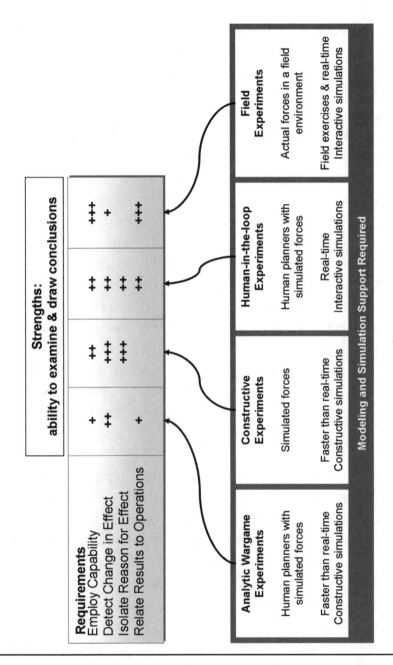

Figure 20. Different Experiment Venues have Different Strengths

limitation is the inability to isolate the true cause of change because of the myriad differences found in attempting to play two different campaigns against a similar reactive threat.

Constructive experiments reflect the closed-loop, force-on-force simulation employed by the modeling and simulation community. In a closed-loop simulation, no human intervention occurs in the play after designers choose the initial parameters and then start and finish the simulation. Constructive simulations are a mainstay of warfighting experimentation that all military analytical agencies employ. Constructive simulations allow repeated replay of the same battle under identical conditions, while systematically varying parameters: the insertion of a new weapon or sensor characteristic, the employment of a different resource or tactic, or the encounter of a different threat. Constructive simulation experiments with multiple runs are ideal to detect change and to isolate its cause. Because modeling complex events requires many assumptions, critics often question the applicability of constructive simulation results to operational situations.

Human-in-the-loop virtual experiments are a blend of constructive experiments and field experiments. The prototype virtual simulation is the flight simulator, where the human pilot makes all the decisions and controls the real-time inputs, while the simulation provides artificial yet realistic real-time feedback. In a command and control human-in-the-loop warfighting experiment, a military staff receives real-time, simulated sensor inputs, makes real-time decisions to manage the battlespace, and directs simulated forces against simulated threat forces. The use of actual military operators and staffs allows this type of experiment to reflect warfighting decisionmaking better than purely closed-loop constructive experiments. However, humans often play differently against computer opponents than against real opponents. Additionally, when humans make decisions, variability increases, and changes are more difficult to detect.

Field experiments are wargames conducted in the actual environment, with actual military units and equipment and with operational prototypes. As such, the results of these experiments are highly applicable to real situations. Good field experiments, like good military exercises, are the closest thing to real military operations. A major advantage of the previous three experiment venues is their ability to examine capabilities that do not yet exist by simulating those capabilities. Field experiments, on the other hand, require working prototypes of new capabilities. Interestingly, while field experiments provide the best opportunity to examine practical representations of these new capabilities, field experiments are also the most difficult environment to employ the new capability. Simultaneously, the new capability has to function and the operators need to know how to employ it. This is a tall order when the new capability will arrive just in time to start trials. Difficulties reside in detecting change and isolating the true cause of any detected change because multiple trials are seldom conducted in field experiments and the trial conditions include much of the uncertainty, variability, and challenges of actual operations.

USING THE FRAMEWORK TO IMPROVE INDIVIDUAL EXPERIMENTS

The following checklist[34] is useful in planning and reviewing warfighting experiments. Experimenters use the column labeled "priority" to indicate how much of a concern a particular threat is to the purpose of the experiment. As will be discussed in the next chapter, different threats are less critical at different stages in the combat development cycle. For the high priority threats, experimenters list appropriate good practices that can be applied to counter the priority threats. The discussion of techniques in Chapters 4 through 7 as well as the summary in Appendix A is relevant for completing this column. The "impact" allows the experimenter to estimate the degree of anticipated success as a result of the application of one or more good practices to counter a particular threat.

---

[34] Thanks to Mr. Michael Wahl at USJFCOM for suggesting this checklist approach and developing an early version.

Checklist for Improving Experiment Validity			
Experiment Threat	Priority	Action	Impact
Ability to Use Capability			
1. Capability functionality does not work. Will the hardware and software work?			
2. Players are not adequately prepared. Do the players have the training and TTPs to use the capability?			
3. Measures are insensitive to capability impact. Is the experiment output sensitive to capability use?			
4. Capability has no opportunity to perform. Does the scenario and Master Scenario Event List (MSEL) call for capability use?			
Ability to Detect Change			
5. Capability systems vary in performance. Are systems (hardware and software) and use in like trials the same?			
6. Experiment players vary in proficiency. Do individual operators/units in like trials have similar characteristics?			
7. Data collection accuracy is inconsistent. Is there large error variability in the data collection process?			
8. Trial conditions fluctuate. Are there uncontrolled changes in trial conditions for like trials?			
9. Sample size is insufficient. Is the analysis efficient and sample sufficient?			
10. Statistical assumptions are violated. Are the correct analysis techniques used and error rate avoided?			
Ability to Isolate Reason for Change: Single Group Design			
11. Functionality changes across trials. Will system (hardware or software) or process change during the test?			
12. Player proficiency changes across trials. Will the player unit change over time?			
13. Data collection accuracy change across trials. Will instrumentation or manual data collection change during the experiment?			
14. Trial conditions change across trials. Will trial conditions (such as weather, light, start conditions, and threat) change during the experiment?			

Checklist for Improving Experiment Validity			
Experiment Threat	Priority	Action	Impact
Ability to Isolate Reason for Change: Multiple Group Design			
15. Groups differ in player proficiency. Are there differences between groups unrelated to the treatment?			
16. Data collection accuracy differs for each group. Are there potential data collection differences between treatment groups?			
17. Groups operate under different trial conditions. Are the trial conditions similar for each treatment group?			
Ability to Relate Results			
18. Functionality does not represent future capability. Is the experimental surrogate functionally representative?			
19. Players do not represent operational unit. Is the player unit similar to the intended operational unit?			
20. Measures do not reflect important effects. Do the performance measures reflect the desired operational outcome?			
21. Scenario is not realistic. Are the Blue, Green, and Red conditions realistic?			

EXPERIMENTING DURING EXERCISES AND OPERATIONS

Individual warfighting experiments may occur during military exercises and operations[35]—mostly during the prototype assessment phase. Early concept experiments are less amenable to exercises and operations because they examine capability variations and tradeoffs where no prototypes exist. Where prototypes are available, the experiment hypotheses would read: *If the unit employs the new prototype or capability, then the unit will be able to accomplish X.*

---

[35] Cebrowski, "Criteria for Successful Experimentation." p. 3.

Although exercises and operations do not allow execution of elaborate experiment designs because it would impede training and impact operational readiness,[36] this validity framework may also be used to improve experiments embedded in real-world exercises. Experimentation during exercises and operations naturally provides the strongest method to meet experiment Requirement 4 (the ability to relate results to actual operations). While operational necessity restricts the ability to meet the first three experiment requirements, the experimenter may diminish the limitations to some degree:

- Requirement 1: Prototype testing prior to the exercise or operation enhances the chance to use the experimental capability and to ensure that it will function during the exercise trials. Additionally, the prototype engineers should train the operators to use the system.
- Requirement 2: To detect change, define *expected performance* before the exercise, and compare the prototype's actual performance during the exercise to its expected performance. Experiment designers may delineate expected performance in terms of "operational sequence diagrams,"[37] or in terms of existing or new tasks, conditions, and standards.
- Requirement 3: The ability to isolate any observed change to the experimental prototype causes the most problems in embedded experimentation. If several capabilities are examined during a single exercise, experimenters should conduct different prototype trials at different times during the exercise so the effects of one prototype do not influence the effects of another. An

[36] Cebrowski, "Criteria for Successful Experimentation." p. 3.
[37] Ibid., p. 2.

experienced exercise "observer–controller (OC)" should view the prototype trial to assess whether observed results emerged from the experimental capability rather than from unintended causes. Additionally, to support Requirement 3, the experimenter should demonstrate that the rigorous experiment data accumulated during the concept development phase of the prototype is still relevant to the exercise conditions. Finally, a model–exercise–model paradigm (see Chapter 10) that was successfully calibrated to the operational exercise results should allow follow-on sensitivity analysis to demonstrate that inclusion and exclusion of the experimental capability accounted for decisive simulation differences.

CHAPTER 9

DESIGNING EXPERIMENTS

WITH MULTIPLE TRIALS

This book is about designing experiments. Experiment design involves choosing a treatment (new capability), deciding how its effect will be measured, constructing and scheduling experiment trials to exercise the capability and produce a measurable observation, and identifying and selecting experiment players to operate the new capability under the trial conditions. This chapter focuses on good practices associated with arranging multiple experiment trials into a cohesive experiment design.

An experiment trial is an opportunity to observe the treatment to see if it produces the hypothesized effect. A trial may be as simple as the presentation of a target to a new sensor to see if it results in detection. The trial may also be as complex as a military staff working together to produce an operational plan. In the former, the trial might last minutes while, in the latter, it may take days to execute.

Most warfighting experiments have multiple trials. That is, the experimenter is interested in seeing how the treatment performs in comparison to alternative capabilities or under different conditions. Single trial experiments occur and are discussed below but they do not provide the rich information found in multiple trial experiments. This chapter presents the pitfalls and techniques for constructing multiple trial experiments. The discussion centers on nine typical warfighting experiment designs to provide templates for practical applications. It will be shown that the threats to validity, especially the threats associated with Experiment Requirement 3, play a dominant role in multiple trial design considerations.

THE CASE FOR MULTIPLE TRIALS IN AN EXPERIMENT

An experiment with multiple trials is valuable to increase sample size, to compare alternative capabilities, and to increase the applicability of the experiment. Experiment sample size is critical to countering Threat 9, a major threat affecting the ability to detect change. Experiment sample size can be increased by increasing the number of trials and by increasing the number of observations within a trial. These ideas will be discussed in detail below.

Multiple trials are also used to examine alternate proposed capability solutions. For example, there may be several sensor technologies proposed to solve a detection problem. The alternative sensors would be examined in separate experiment trials. Is some cases, a proposed new system is compared to the current system. In this instance, the trial with the current capability is called the *baseline* trial.

The third reason for multiple trials is to specifically examine additional scenario conditions within the potential operational envelope of the new capability. For example, the new sensor capability could be examined against an alternate sensor in a wide range of target altitudes. Each different combination (sensor by altitude) would represent a separate designed experiment trial. To examine two different sensors at three different target altitudes would require six trials. Examining the operational envelope of a capability is a good practice to counter Threat 21 and supports the ability to relate results to the operational environment.

The notion of employing multiple trials and multiple observations within a trial to increase sample size are discussed first. To do this, some new experimentation terminology is introduced. The final portions of this chapter provide examples and discussion on good techniques for designing multiple experiment trials to examine alternative treatments and alternative conditions.

EXPERIMENT TRIAL LANGUAGE

A specific vocabulary has evolved to communicate the organization of trials and sample size in an experiment. This terminology includes such terms as factors, conditions, cells, replications, trials, and sample size. Figure 21 provides an example of how these terms are combined in an experiment design. Experiment factors represent the primary treatment variables. The experiment design matrix in Figure 21 has two factors: sensors and target altitude. Experiment conditions[38] describe subdivisions within the primary factors. In this exam-

---

[38] The conditions of an experiment factor are also referred to as *levels*.

	Target Altitude		
	Low	Medium	High
Sensor J	R2	R3	R2
Sensor K	R2	R3	R2

Figure 21. Example of Factorial Experiment Design Matrix

ple, the sensor factor has two conditions (Sensor J and Sensor K) and the target altitude factor has three conditions (low, medium, and high).

The factors and conditions in this experiment represent a factorial experiment. *Factorial* means that there are at least two factors, each having more than one condition; and the conditions for one factor are "crossed" with the conditions from the other factor, thus yielding condition combinations. The Sensor J condition is completely crossed with the altitude conditions in that Sensor J will be examined under all three altitude conditions.

EXPERIMENT TRIALS AND SAMPLE SIZE

The design matrix in Figure 21 has six experiment trials representing the six factorial combinations of sensor and target conditions.[39] The number of experiment observations in each cell are called *replications* and are represented as R2 (two observations) and R3 (three observations). The total number of replications determines the total sample size or total number of observations, which total 14 in this example. Individual

[39] Each combination, each cell, represents a particular experiment "treatment combination."

experiment cells may have a different number of replications. In this example, the medium altitude condition is to be examined three times for each sensor because it is the most likely scenario condition. The two other altitudes will be examined only twice for each sensor to save resources.

Chapter 5 discusses the value of increasing sample size to increase the ability to detect change. How big should the sample size be: 4, 10, 30, or 100? Standard statistical textbooks provide formulas for computing the minimum sample size required to detect a specific difference between two alternatives. It is not always possible to design warfighting experiments with sufficient trials to achieve required sample sizes due to resource constraints. This is why Chapter 5 provides considerable discussion on variance reduction methods involving the treatment, experiment unit, and measurement devices. Variance reduction techniques along with increases in sample size contribute to reducing experiment noise so that the experiment signal (potential differences between alternative treatments) can be detected.

While it may appear that warfighting experiments always have low sample sizes, there are occasions when a larger number of replications is available to meet sample size requirements. The surest way to design sufficient replications into the experiment occurs in constructive simulation experiments. This is accomplished by executing stochastic replications after the simulation base case is established. In simulation experiments, it is quite easy to run 10 or even 30 replications for each experiment matrix cell. This is one reason why constructive simulation experiments are so adept at providing statistically defensible results.

A large number of pre-determined replications can also be obtained in virtual and field experiments when the experiment unit is an individual or small team. For example, suppose 300 soldiers or Marine riflemen were available to examine the effects of a new capability on individual marksmanship. If the experiment matrix in Figure 21 represented two different rifle scopes to be examined at three different ranges, 50 riflemen could be assigned to each of the six experiment cells. If each rifleman produces a single score, then each cell has 50 replications and the experiment has an overall sample size of 300.

A third way to obtain a large sample size is to design a longer-duration trial for each of the six cells in Figure 21. During a particular trial execution, an experiment unit would be given the opportunity to execute a short-duration task a number of times and each time the task was attempted it would be recorded as a replication. For example, Sensor J team might be presented with 30 different targets during an 8-hour trial. The targets could be randomly presented at low, medium, and high altitudes during the extended trial. At the end of the trial, Sensor J (first row in Figure 21) would have 30 replications distributed across its three columns, with 8-12 replications in any one of its three experiment cells.

MULTIPLE TRIAL DESIGN CONSIDERATIONS

Sample size was only one of the three reasons given above for multiple trials in experiments. Trials generated for sample size alone focus on replicating more of the same to enhance detection of differences. The remainder of this chapter focuses on the art of designing multiple trials to examine alternative capabilities or environments. The following discussion is an adaptation of the basic designs discussed in Chapters 4 through 8 in Shadish, Cook, and Campbell (2002). Nine prototypical warfighting experiment designs are discussed.

Single Group Experiment Designs

- Single Trial Design
- Single Trial Design with Pre-Test
- Two Trial Design with a Baseline
- Design with Two or More Trials to Compare Alternatives
- Factorial Design

Multiple Group Experiment Designs

- Two Trial Design
- Two Trial Design with Pre-Test
- Design with Crossover Group
- Factorial Design

In each instance, the basic design is presented to show how it is used in warfighting experimentation. This is followed by a discussion of the strengths and weaknesses of the design with respect to the four experiment requirements. While these nine designs do not cover all of the possibilities and variations, the discussion is intended to acquaint the reader with a strategy for considerations when developing an experiment design for their own research problem.

SINGLE GROUP EXPERIMENT DESIGNS

Recall from Chapter 7 that single group designs are experiments that employ just one player group (one staff element, one squad, one company, one cell, one team, etc.) during the entire experiment. However, single group design does not mean a single observation design. Single group designs can generate any number of observations (replications) during an experiment trial. One way is to observe individual members of the team performing individual tasks, for example, attempting to locate adversaries in a particular geographical region. Each time an individual in the group attempts a task, it is counted as an observation. A second way to generate replications is to have the group work as a unit to accomplish a series of unit tasks a number of times during the trial. Thus, single trial designs do not mean single sample size events, but rather that a single group of participants is providing all of the information in the experiment.

Single Trial Design

The simplest form of the single *group* experiment is the single *trial* experiment illustrated in Figure 22. Single trial experiments typically involve taking an available unit and giving them a new piece of equipment (usually a prototype), new procedures, or new organization and observing the extent to which they accomplish a task. These are "one-shot" designs. Requirements 2 and 3 are very difficult to meet in this design.

This design can only satisfy Requirement 2 (detect a difference) when there is a well-established threshold as depicted in Figure 23. Established thresholds (or criteria) are rare. Sometimes pre-established thresholds are available from historical knowledge. For example, prior to 1947 no one had flown faster than the speed of sound. Pre-existing thresholds are also available in the military acquisition arena where a system must

Figure 22. Single Trial Experiment Design Matrix

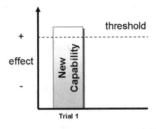

Figure 23. Single Trial Data Display

meet a specific threshold (for example, fire so many rounds per minute) before the system will be funded.

When thresholds are not available, a technique often employed is to survey or interview the participants for their opinions as to the extent that the new capability enabled them to achieve the task better than if they had attempted the task without the new capability. While one cannot discount professionals with many years of experience, it does not bear the same conclusiveness that measurement to a threshold standard does.

Even when task accomplishment can be measured with some objectivity (such as the number of targets detected) and this measurement can be compared to an objective predetermined threshold, it will be difficult to ascertain why the threshold was accomplished. Could the task have been accomplished without employing the new capability? Perhaps the task and threshold are not that difficult to achieve. On the other hand, perhaps it is difficult, but the participants had rehearsed it so often in the pre-experiment training that it became artificially easy for them. In this design it is virtually impossible to isolate the reason for change. The experimenter can survey the participants and external observers for their rationales for task accomplishment, but often conflicting rationales are given.

Single Trial Design with a Pre-Test

When objective thresholds and control groups are not available, there may be an opportunity to include a pre-test in the single trial experiment as illustrated in Figure 24. This single group design often occurs in the training environment where achievement scores from a gunnery range, flight simulator, or physical fitness test are available. In these experiments, participants with scores are chosen to participate in an experiment designed to improve performance. At the end of the trial, participants are evaluated against the same task as the pre-test and the pre- and post-scores are compared (see Figure 25). An improvement from the pre-test to the post-trial would indicate that the new capability improved their performance.

While this design provides the ability to detect change, if change occurs, the design will have problems in isolating the reason for change. It is quite possible that the experience of taking the pre-test was sufficient training in itself to improve performance on the post-test without the additional experimental training.

An additional threat to isolating change occurs when participants are chosen for the experiment based on their pre-test performance. Often in experiments involving new training

Group 1		Trial 1
	Pre-Test	New Capability

Figure 24. Single Trial Design Matrix with a Pre-Test

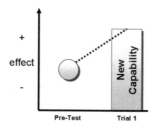

Figure 25. Single Trial Design with Pre-Test Data Display

devices, only participants who scored low on the pre-test are assigned to the experimental training system. The danger in this assignment strategy is that participants with low pre-test sores tend to automatically show improvement on the post-trial test even with no additional training. Individuals with low pre-test scores will naturally exhibit higher post-experiment scores while individuals with high initial pre-experiment scores will naturally exhibit lower post-experiment scores. This shift towards the middle of the score range (regression towards the mean) occurs in the absence of any intervention and is a result of the measurement error in the pre-experiment testing. Consequently, players assigned to a training condition based on low scores will show an improvement even if the new training system is irrelevant to performance.

To reduce this risk, establish a control group. Operators with low pre-experiment scores would be assigned randomly to two

	Trial 1	Trial 2
Group 1	Current capability (baseline)	New Capability

Figure 26. Two Trial Design Matrix with a Baseline in the First Trial

groups: a control group and the new training group. The control group would not participate in any remedial training. While both groups will show improvement upon retesting, if the new training group shows more improvement than the control group, a case can be made for the utility of the new training system.

Single Group Two Trial Design with a Baseline

Pre-testing is not an option for most warfighting experiments. The more typical design is a two trial experiment with one trial serving as the baseline condition (Figure 26). In Trial 1, participants execute the experiment task without the benefit of the new capability. This is the experiment baseline. Trial 2 is executed after the same participants are trained on the new capability. If Trial 2 shows an increase in performance over Trial 1, experimenters would like to conclude that this was a result of the new capability. Unfortunately, this conclusion is difficult to defend in this two trial design and in some cases may be the wrong conclusion.

There is no way to determine whether the improvement from Trial 1 to 2 was solely a result of the participants' practicing the task in the baseline trial. This learning effect (Threat 12) may have led to improved performance in Trial 2, even with-

	Trial 1	Trial 2
Group 1	New capability	Current Capability (baseline)

Figure 27. Two Trial Design Matrix with a Baseline in the Second Trial

out the new capability. Threat 12 to Requirement 3 is discussed in detail in Chapter 6.

One counter to Threat 12 is to conduct the baseline during the second trial as illustrated in Figure 27. In this design, participants are immediately trained on the new capability and use it first in Trial 1. The new capability is then taken away and they execute Trial 2. Now if performance is higher in Trial 1 than Trial 2, the experimenter can rule out practice and experience. Any learning effects would have helped the baseline trial, not the new capability trial.

The technique of reversing experiment trials by executing the baseline trial following the new capability trial exemplifies the difference between an experiment and training exercise. In training the best practice is to crawl, walk, and run because the trainer is concerned with task accomplishment. Accordingly, the trainer conducts the more familiar trial first followed by the less familiar. The experimenter is also concerned with task accomplishment, but is more concerned with comparing the effectiveness of one solution to another. To do this, the experimenter needs to eliminate alternative explanations for performance differences.

Conducting the baseline trial second offers a much stronger case for concluding that the primary reason for better perfor-

	Trial 1	Trial 2	Trial 3
Group 1	Capability J	Capability K	Capability L

Figure 28. Design Matrix to Compare Alternatives

mance during Trial 1 was the new capability. However, the design is not perfect. The experimenter still has to rule out that the lower performance in Trial 2 was not due to fatigue or boredom.

Single Group Design with Two or More Trials to Compare Alternatives

A variation of the two trial baseline design is the use of two or more trials to compare alternative capabilities when none of the alternatives is considered a baseline or control condition. These experiments tend not to have thresholds and are interested in only obtaining a "relative measure of merit." While experimenters cannot say if any one of the new capabilities meets a threshold, experimenters would like to determine if one is better than another. These sound plausible, unfortunately without a control group, the design depicted in Figure 28 has a difficult time living up to expectations.

If the different trials represent similar problems under different conditions, the data can be represented as in Figure 29. It is not easy to interpret these results. The experimenter would like to say that Capability K was best, followed by L and J. Once again, however, this conclusion would not be easy to support because it is difficult to isolate the reason for change. The results for Capability J and K could be explained by learning effects (Threat 12).

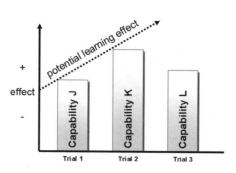

Figure 29. Alternative Comparison Design Data Display

If the results had shown a consistent increase from Trial 1 through Trial 3, one would be suspicious of consistent learning effects. It is difficult to understand what happened in Trial 3. Is the decrease from Trial 2 due to the inferiority of Capability L to K? Or is the decrease due to something else? Perhaps the task in Trial 3 was more difficult than Trial 2.

In single group alternative-comparison designs, the biggest problem is overcoming the learning effects associated with conducting sequential trials with the same group. This learning effects threat was illustrated previously in Chapter 6, Figure 15. When one capability is considered the baseline, the experimenter can counter the learning threat by scheduling the baseline trial last as in Figure 27. Unfortunately, reversing trials is not an option when none of the capabilities is considered the baseline.

A technique to counter Threat 12 for alternative comparisons is to run more trials than alternatives. Example results of such a design are illustrated in Figure 30. Notice that the trials are counterbalanced. It is easier to believe that learning effects are

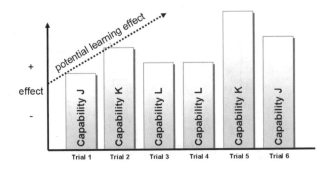

Figure 30. Comparison Design with Additional Trials

	Problem X		Problem Y	
	Threat 1	Threat 2	Threat 1	Threat 2
New Capability	Group 1 (trial 2)	Group 1 (trial 4)	Group 1 (trial 6)	Group 1 (trial 7)
Current Capability	Group 1 (trial 8)	Group 1 (trial 3)	Group 1 (trial 5)	Group 1 (trial 1)

Figure 31. Single Group Factorial Design Matrix

less dominant in Trials 4, 5, and 6. One could more safely conclude that Capability K was consistently better than J and L.

Single Group Factorial Design

This design is an elaboration of the single group alternate comparison design to assess alternative capabilities under multiple
conditions in one experiment as shown in Figure 31. This type
of design only works when trials can be conducted in a short
duration, the participants can switch from one situation to
another (trial conditions) with minimum cognitive disruption,
and there are minimal learning effects from trial to trial. When
learning effects are expected, it is critical to run the eight experi-

	Problem X		Problem Y	
	Threat 1	Threat 2	Threat 1	Threat 2
New Capability	Group 1 (trial 2)			Group 1 (trial 3)
Current Capability		Group 1 (trial 1)	Group 1 (trial 4)	

Figure 32. Single Group Fractional-Factorial Design Matrix

ment trials in a random order. One possible trial execution sequence is provided in Figure 31 as trial 1 through trial 8.

The advantage of the factorial design is the ability to examine interaction effects. Are there constant differences between the new and current capability? Or does the difference in effectiveness of the two capabilities depend on (interact with) the type of problem attempted or the threat levels? If the magnitude of the difference between the two capabilities varies under the different conditions, then there is an interaction between the capabilities factor and the other two factors (problem and threat). This 3-factor analysis of variance design requires eight different trials to execute a single replication in each cell.

The disadvantage of factorial designs is that they can require a large number of trials. The 3-factor design in Figure 31 requires eight trials. It is possible to execute fractional-factorial experiment designs that require fewer trials. The example in Figure 32 requires only four trials instead of eight. The tradeoff is that the experimenter forfeits the ability to examine many of the potential interaction effects and focuses primarily on the main effects. Fractional-factorial designs are useful for examining a larger number of factors with the least number of trials.

Factorial designs are quite common in constructive simulation experiments. They are often difficult to execute in virtual or field experiments due to the requirement for shorter trials and the absence of strong learning effects from one trial to the next. They work best when the experiment subjects have mastered the training curve and any variability in their performance can be attributed to the quality of their tools (new versus current capability) or the difficulty of the conditions imposed (problem type and threat level).

MULTIPLE GROUP EXPERIMENT DESIGNS

Multiple group designs are experiments that employ two or more player groups. Sometimes the second group operates an alternative capability. Most often however, the second player group is required to operate the current capability system or baseline system. In this case, the group is called the *control group*.

Multiple group designs bring with them a special consideration not found for single group designs. That is, how to assign participants to the different groups? There are two options: randomly assigned or not randomly assigned. How participants are assigned to the different experiment groups greatly impacts the ability to isolate the reason for any observed differences in performance. The second option will be discussed first.

Non-Random Assignment to Groups

Most warfighting experiments assign participants to different experiment groups based on non-random considerations. When a number of individuals or teams are available for assignment to two or more treatment conditions, they are often placed in experimental groups reflecting their current organizational grouping because they have experience in working together as a team, platoon, squadron, staff, or ship.

Experiment designs with non-random assignment to groups were first described in detail by Campbell and Stanley in 1963. The lack of random assignment exacerbates player differences (Threat 15) and makes it extremely difficult to identify the reason for any change (Requirement 3). Experiments where participants are not assigned to groups randomly are called *quasi-experiment designs.*[40]

Random Assignment to Groups

It is the rare warfighting experiment where available military personnel can be randomly assigned to alternative experiment groups. When this occurs, the experiment is considered a randomized experiment.[41]

The usual practice of random assignment can occur as follows. All of the individuals or teams available for the experiment are listed in some order, say alphabetically. The experimenter flips a coin for each available participant: heads, the participant goes to Group 1; and tails, the participant goes to Group 2. While the process is simple, it is the most powerful technique for countering the dominant threat to isolating the reason for change in multiple group experiments. The dominant threat is Threat 15. When experiment groups are developed non-randomly, one can never be sure if the experiment results were due to differences in capabilities or due to differences in the composition of the experiment groups. Is one group more

---

[40] Shadish et al., *Experimental and Quasi-Experimental Designs.* p. 12.

[41] Ibid., p. 12.

Design with a Control Group		Design with an Alternative Group	
	Trials		**Trials**
Group 1	New Capability (trial 1)	Group 1	New Capability 1 (trial 1)
Group 2 (control)	Current Capability (trial 2)	Group 2 (alternate)	New Capability 2 (trial 2)

Figure 33. Multiple Group Two Trial Design Matrices

experienced and motivated than the other? Randomization acts to equally divide these influences between the groups.

As pointed out earlier however, random assignment is not always desirable even if possible. When two different integral units become available for an experiment, randomly assigning the individuals to one group or the other would jeopardize the integrity, training, and efficiency of unit performance. Based on the nature of the task in the experiment, the experimenter has to make a difficult choice as to whether to maintain the unit integrity for efficiency or employ randomization to better isolate the reason for experiment differences. The implications of this decision (employing randomized or non-randomized assignment to groups) will be discussed for each of the multiple group designs.

Multiple Group Two Trial Design

There are two variations in the multiple group two trial design depicted in Figure 33. When the second group executes the identical task with the current capability, the second group is a *control group*. If the second group employs an alternate capability, it is an *alternate group*.

Compare this control group design to the comparable single group design in Figure 26 and this alternate group design to Figure 27. In multiple group designs, control and alternative group variations can be discussed together because the threats and counters are similar. In multiple group designs, the application of good techniques does not depend on whether the *second group* employs a current (baseline) system or an alternate system. By contrast, in the single group design we learned that different techniques were available when the *second trial* was a baseline trial rather than an alternate-system trial.

In this multiple group two trial design, it makes no difference which trial is executed first. In fact, they could be executed simultaneously in different locations. Less apparent, but critical to interpreting results, is that the tasks to be accomplished by the two different groups in Figure 33 can be—and should be—identical. In the single group designs, the scenario problems cannot be identical because the group would respond from memory in subsequent trials. Thus, the experimenter has to develop "equivalent but not identical" scenario problems. This is not always easy.

At first glance, one might conclude that multiple group experiments are superior to single group experiments in interpreting differences because there is no "trial sequence" problem. If Group 1 did better, it had to be due to the capability they employed. That is the only difference in the experiment. Similarly, if there is no difference between groups, then there is no difference between capabilities employed by the two groups.

Not so fast. These conclusions are warranted only if the individuals had been assigned to the two groups randomly. This is not a strong design if participants are not randomly assigned to

		Trials
Group 1	Pre-Test	New Capability (trial 1)
Group 2 (control)	Pre-Test	Current Capability (trial 2)

Figure 34. Multiple Group Pre-Test Design Matrix

treatment conditions. By now, the reader knows that inherent differences in the original (non-randomized) groups could be the dominant reason for performance differences. This problem is discussed extensively in Chapter 6 as Threat 15. The next two designs are variations to specifically help ameliorate Threat 15.

Multiple Group Two Trial Design with a Pre-Test

When random assignment is not an option, the use of a pre-test will help isolate the reason for change. The multiple group two trial design with a pre-test can be displayed as in Figure 34. As discussed previously for the comparable single group design, pre-tests are usually available in the training environment. In this case, the pre-test scores are used to indicate the extent to which the two groups are equivalent at the start of the experiment.

The best case is when the pre-test indicates no difference between the two groups prior to the trials as illustrated on the left in Figure 35. This gives supporting evidence that any improvements demonstrated by the new capability group (G-1) can be attributed to the new capability.

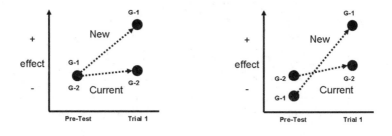

**Figure 35. Multiple Group Two Trial Design Matrices
with Pre-Test Data Displays**

The experiment interpretation is problematic when the pre-test scores indicate that the two groups are not equivalent. If Group 1's pre-scores are better than Group 2's, any subsequent improved performance by Group 1 can be interpreted as occurring because they started ahead. Conversely, if Group 1's pre-scores are worse than Group 2's (example on the right in Figure 35), a logical case can be made that Group 1's improvement during the experiment trial was due to the new capability. However, it is not as strong a case as when they both performed equally on the pre-test. The experimenter would still be concerned with the "John Henry effect" in Threat 15. Perhaps Group 1 knew they had not done as well on the pre-test and their improvement was due to increased motivation, not the new capability.

Multiple Group Design with Cross-Over Group

Instead of using a pre-test, the experimenter can directly tackle the problem of non-randomized groups by employing a cross-over experiment design. In this design, both Groups have the opportunity to employ the new capability and baseline current

	Trials	Trials
Group 1	Current Capability (trial 1)	New Capability (trial 3)
Group 2 (control)	New Capability (trial 2)	Current Capability (trial 4)

Figure 36. Multiple Group Cross-Over Design Matrix

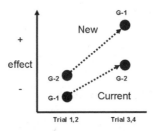

Figure 37. Multiple Group Cross-Over Design Display

capability as illustrated in Figure 36. Each group acts as its own control. If one group is inherently better than the other, the experimenter can still examine whether the new capability improves performance for each group separately.

This cross-over design also allows the experimenter to measure the impact of learning effects from the first series of trials (trial 1 and 2) to the second series (trial 3 and 4). Notice in the example data display in Figure 37 that both groups (G-1 and G-2) show improvement from initial trials to follow-on trials. This suggests that the initial practice had a strong impact. However, the new capability showed consistent improvement for both trials indicating that the effectiveness of the new capability was sufficient to overcome the learning effect.

	Problem X		Problem Y	
	Threat 1	Threat 2	Threat 1	Threat 2
New Capability	Group 1	Group 2	Group 3	Group 4
Current Capability	Group 5	Group 6	Group 7	Group 8

Figure 38. Multiple Group Factorial Design Matrix

While the cross-over is a powerful design for non-randomized groups, there are practical problems in applicability. Half of the experiment time and resources will be devoted to the baseline condition, allowing less time for a more in-depth examination of the new capability. Both groups require new capability training, which requires more training resources.

Multiple Group Factorial Designs

The multiple group factorial designs look just like the single group factorial designs with one exception. Each cell in this factorial design has a different group. Compare the multiple group factorial design in Figure 38 with the previous single group factorial design in Figure 31. In the multiple group design, the experimenter requires as many different groups as there are matrix cells. This is easier to do when each group represents a small unit, for example: different fire teams or squads from a larger unit, individual vehicles, aircraft sorties, or patrol boats. The fractional-factorial designs, as discussed previously in Figure 32, are also available in the multiple group variation.

The advantage of the multiple group factorial design over the single group design is that the sequence of trials is no longer an issue. In many cases, the experiment trials can be presented simultaneously to several groups at a time in different geographical areas. There are two primary disadvantages. First, multiple groups have to be available and trained, which is a resource limitation. More importantly, however, the experimenter needs to be very concerned about countering Threat 15—the possibility that the individual groups in each cell are inherently different prior to the experiment.

The best counter to Threat 15 is to randomly assign individual elements to the group in each cell. As discussed above, this works best when experimenters have a large number of individual "experiment elements," let us say 40 marksmen or 40 vehicles with drivers, and can randomly assign 5 of the 40 to each of the 8 groups in Figure 37. This only works when "group integrity" is not a primary consideration. The initial equivalence of experimental groups is the primary concern in a multiple group factorial design of warfighting experiments with human participants. Factorial experiments work quite easily in constructive simulations because the simulations can be made equivalent in each cell except for the cell conditions.

SUMMARY COMMENTS

Designing individual warfighting experiments is an art. These first 10 chapters discuss the many considerations, tradeoffs, and decisions in this art. I call it an art because every experiment is a compromise. The logical framework in the preceding chapters is designed to assist the experimenter in understanding the choices available and the interactions and impacts of these choices. The next chapter will discuss how these choices also apply to designing a campaign of experiments in order to examine a problem through multiple related experiments.

CHAPTER 10

IMPROVING EXPERIMENT CAMPAIGNS

EMPLOYING MULTIPLE EXPERIMENT METHODS TO INCREASE RIGOR

A campaign of experiments can consist of a number of successive, individual experiments to fully examine proposed solutions to complex military problems. It can also consist of a set of experiments conducted in parallel with information and findings passed back and forth. All military experimenters agree on the usefulness of experiment campaigns. This chapter provides an overarching framework for planning the sequence of experiments to enhance the validity of the final recommendations.

A campaign of experiments can accumulate validity across the four requirements.

> This [long list of validity threats] might lead readers to wonder if any single experiment can successfully avoid

all of them. The answer is no. We cannot reasonably expect one study to deal with all of them simultaneously, primarily because of logical and practical tradeoffs among them.... It is more realistic to expect a program of research to deal with most or all of these threats over time. Knowledge growth is more cumulative than episodic, both with experiments and with any type of research.[42]

This chapter initially examines the more general situation of designing experiment campaigns to match the combat development cycle requirements, from exploring concepts to fielding prototypes. The chapter then turns to a specific experimentation campaign paradigm—the model-wargame-model paradigm (M-W-M)—in which constructive experiments and wargame experiments are combined to make up for the validity deficiencies by either when in isolation.

EMPHASIZING DIFFERENT EXPERIMENT REQUIREMENTS DURING CONCEPT DEVELOPMENT AND EXPERIMENTATION (CDE)

A comprehensive CDE campaign should include a series of individual experiments that emphasize different experiment requirements. Figure 39 illustrates one example of a CDE campaign. The campaign starts at the top with discovery activities and proceeds to the bottom with capability implementation into the joint force. Each step in the campaign identifies possible experimentation goals. On the right of the experimentation goals, the "pluses" portray the relative importance of the four

---

[42] Shadish et al., *Experimental and Quasi-Experimental Designs.* p. 96.

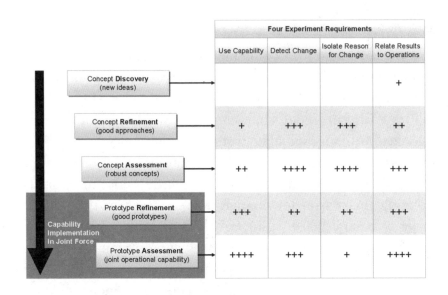

Figure 39. Experiment Campaign Requirements during Concept and Prototype Development

validity requirements for that experimentation step. The following discussion identifies possible experiment venues that can be employed at each CDE step to address the goals and validity requirements.

Concept Discovery

The primary consideration during concept discovery is relevance and comprehensiveness. To what extent do initial articulations of the future operational environment include a comprehensive description of the expected problems and propose a full set of relevant solutions? Relevancy, however, should not be over-stressed. It is important to avoid eliminating unanticipated or unexpected results that subsequent experimentation could investigate further.

Emphasizing Different Experiment Requirements during Concept Development and Experimentation (CDE)

Concept Refinement

Finding an initial set of potential capabilities that empirically show promise is most important in concept refinement. These early experiments examine idealized capabilities (future capabilities with projected characteristics) to determine whether they lead to increased effectiveness. Initial concept refinement experiments are dependent on simulations to represent simulated capabilities in simulated environments. Accurately isolating the reason for change is less critical at this stage in order to permit "false positives." Allowing some false solutions to progress and be examined in later experiments under more realistic environments is more important than eliminating potential solutions too quickly. Concept refinement is dependent on the simulation-supported experiment such as constructive, analytic wargame, and human-in-the-loop experiments. Sometimes simple field experiments can be constructed to investigate whether future technologies will lead to dramatic differences in operations by employing highly abstract surrogates, for example, designating that a hand-held clipboard provides exact enemy locations.

Concept Assessment

Quantifying operational improvements and correctly identifying the responsible capabilities are paramount in providing evidence for concept acceptance. Concept justification is also dependent on experiments with better defined capabilities across multiple realistic environments. Constructive experiments can provide statistically defensible evidence of improvements across a wide range of conditions. Human-in-the-loop and field experiments with realistic surrogates in realistic operational environments can provide early evidence for capability usability and relevance. Incorporation of the human decisionmaker into human-in-the-loop and field experiments is essential to the concept development process. Early in the concept development process, the human operators tend to find new ways to solve problems.

Prototype Refinement

In prototype experiments, one should anticipate large effects or the implementation might not be cost effective. Accordingly, the experiment can focus on the usability of working prototypes in a realistic experiment environment. Isolating the real cause of change is still critical when improving prototypes. The experiment must be able to isolate the contributions of training, user characteristics, scenario, software, and operational procedures to prototype improvements in order to refine the right component. Human-in-the-loop and field experiments with realistic surrogates in realistic operational environments provide the experimental context for assessing gains in effectiveness when considering capability refinements and employment issues. Human decisionmakers find unexpected ways to use and employ new technologies effectively.

Prototype Assessment

Applicability to the warfighting operational environment is paramount in prototype assessment. If the capability is difficult to use or the desired gains are not readily apparent in the operational environment, it will be difficult to convince the combatant commander to employ it. Uncovering the exact causal chain is less important. In prototype validation, human decisionmakers ensure that the new technology can be employed effectively. Prototype validation experiments are often embedded within joint exercises and operations.

MODEL-WARGAME-MODEL EXPERIMENT CAMPAIGN

When large wargames and large field exercises are used as an experiment to investigate the effectiveness of new capabilities, the results are often disappointing. Because these exercises are player-resource intensive, there are few opportunities to examine alternative capabilities or alternative situations that would allow meaningful comparisons. The model-exercise-model paradigm can enhance the usefulness of wargames and exercises. This paradigm consists of conducting early constructive simulation experiments prior to the wargame or exercise and then following these events with a second set of post-exercise constructive experiments.

Pre-event Constructive Simulation

Early constructive simulation experiments use the same Blue and Red forces anticipated to be played in the exercise. This pre-event simulation examines multiple alternative Blue force capability configurations against different Red force situations. This allows experimenters to determine the most robust Blue force configuration across the different Red force scenarios. It also helps to focus the exercise by pinpointing potential critical junctures to be observed during the follow-on exercise.

Wargame or Exercise Event

The wargame or exercise executes the best Blue force configuration identified during the pre-event simulation. The "best

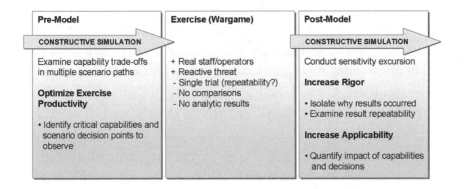

Figure 40. Model-Wargame-Model Campaign

configuration" is one where the simulation indicated that the new capability dramatically improved Blue's outcome. The exercise with independent and reactive Blue and Red force decisionmakers reexamines this optimal configuration and scenario. The scenario that provides the best opportunity for the new capabilities to succeed is chosen because exercises include the "fog of war" and traditionally the experimental capability does not perform as well in the real environment as it does in the simulation. Therefore, it makes sense to give the new capability its best chance to succeed. If it does not succeed in a scenario designed to allow it to succeed, it most likely would not succeed in other scenarios.

Post-event Constructive Simulation

Experimenters use the exercise results to calibrate the original constructive simulation for further post-event simulation analysis. Calibration involves the adjustment of the simulation inputs and parameters to better match the play of the simulation to the play of the wargame. This adds credibility to the simulation. Rerunning the pre-event alternatives in the calibrated model provides a more credible interpretation of any differences now observed in the simulation. Additionally, the post-event calibrated simulation can substantiate (or not) the implications of the wargame recommendations by conducting causal analysis. Causal analysis is a series of "what if" sensitivity simulation runs in the simulation to determine whether the wargame recommendations make a difference in the calibrated simulation outcome. Experimenters can also examine what might have occurred if the Red or Blue forces had made different decisions during the wargame.

SUMMARY

A comprehensive CDE campaign includes a series of individual experiments, each emphasizing different experiment requirements at different stages during the capability development process. In this campaign, no single experiment is expected to carry the entire weight of the decision. Each experiment contributes and the final implementation decision is based on accumulated confidence in the capability as a result of a well-designed mutually supporting campaign of experiments where each experiment contributes its strengths to the final decision. The model–wargame–model paradigm is one example of mutually supporting experiments to increase overall decision validity. It does this by combining a constructive experiment's ability to detect differences among alternative treatments with a wargame or field experiment's ability to incorporate human decisions, which better reflects actual operations. In this paradigm, the whole is better that either part.

APPENDIX A

SUMMARY OF

GOOD EXPERIMENT TECHNIQUES

This section summarizes the good practice counters to the 21 threats to experiment validity displayed in Figure 41. This list is not a "cook book" solution to designing an experiment. The discussion in Chapter 9 demonstrates that it is impossible to satisfy all four experiment requirements simultaneously because the requirements seek to achieve contradictory goals in warfighting experiments: maximization of experiment precision and control works against the ability to maximize free play and realism. An understanding of the logical framework presented in the previous chapters guides the experimenter towards knowledgeable and rational tradeoffs among the good practices to increase experiment rigor.

These techniques are selective. They only pertain to the threats to experiment validity. Good practices involving the mechanics of agency organization, planning, and reporting of

Experiment Components	Experiment Requirements				
	1. Ability to Use the Capability	2. Ability to Detect Change	3. Ability to Isolate the Reason for Change		4. Ability to Relate the Results to Operations
			Single Group	Multiple Groups	
1. Treatment	(1) Capability functionality does not work.	(5) Capability systems vary in performance.	(11) Functionality changes across trials.		(18) Functionality does not represent future capability.
2. Players	(2) Players are not adequately prepared.	(6) Experiment players vary in proficiency.	(12) Player proficiency changes across trials.	(15) Groups differ in player proficiency.	(19) Players do not represent operational unit.
3. Effect	(3) Measures are insensitive to capability impact.	(7) Data collection accuracy is inconsistent.	(13) Data collection accuracy changes across trials.	(16) Data collection accuracy differs for each group.	(20) Measures do not reflect important effects.
4. Trial	(4) Capability has no opportunity to perform.	(8) Trial conditions fluctuate.	(14) Trial conditions change across trials.	(17) Groups operate under different trial conditions.	(21) Scenario is not realistic.
5. Analysis		(9) Sample size is insufficient. (10) Statistical assumptions are violated.			

Figure 41. Twenty-One Threats to a Valid Experiment

experiments are critically important to the success of an experimentation program, but are not included here. However,
agency practices for including stakeholders, holding peer
reviews, using experienced experimenters, and allocating sufficient time and resources to plan, execute, and report an
experiment can counter known threats to the four experiment
requirements by fostering valid experiment designs.

The following techniques are not exhaustive. They provide
examples and aides to better understand the 21 threats to
experiment validity. Understanding the specific threats and
their importance to the logic of warfighting experimentation
allows the experimenter "on the ground" to be creative in
finding more innovative methods for countering specific
threats. Each experiment agency already has lists of useful
experiment practices. These lists of good practices by experienced practitioners can now be partitioned to reinforce and
expand the techniques provided below.

While the experiment requirements are numbered from 1 to 4
and the threats from 1 to 21, this does not imply a priority. The
four requirements represent a *logical*, progressive sequence
within themselves. If each successive requirement is not met in
sequence, there is no need to proceed to the next one. In practice, however, the experimenter considers the interaction
impacts among all four when designing the experiment. Similarly, the threat presentation order does not denote priority. The
military environment traditionally views the appropriateness of
the scenario (Threat 21), the representativeness of the experiment players (Threat 19), and the availability of the
experimental capability (Threat 1) with its operational procedures (Threat 2) as the most critical elements in an exercise. The

following list of good practices indicates that a well-constructed, rigorous experiment requires additional considerations.

TECHNIQUES TO COUNTER THREATS TO REQUIREMENT 1: ABILITY TO USE THE NEW CAPABILITY

Threat 1: New capability functionality does not work.

- Schedule frequent demonstrations of the new capability prior to the experiment. These demonstrations should take place in the experiment environment.
- Prior to the experiment, ensure that new command, control, and communications (C3) systems interoperate with the other systems in the experiment. Systems that interoperated in the designer's facility almost surely will not when brought to the experiment.

Threat 2: Experiment players are not adequately prepared to use the new capability to its fullest extent.

- Provide sufficient practice time for players to be able to operate and optimally employ the system. Not only does the new functionality need to be available ahead of time, but also the tactics, techniques, and procedures and standard operating procedures need to be developed concurrently with the new capability and be available prior to the pilot test.

Threat 3: Experiment measures are insensitive to new capability impact.

- Conduct full-dress rehearsal pilot tests prior to the start of experiment trials to ensure that the experimental capability in the hands of the user can produce the anticipated outcome. If one does not see indications of performance differences between the old and new capability during the pilot test, the trial scenario should be re-examined to see if it sufficiently emphasizes the operational envelope of the new capability.
- If the experiment is to examine different levels of the capability (or the same capability under different conditions) increase the differential between the different levels or different conditions in order to increase the chance of seeing a difference in experiment outcome. However, do not stretch the conditions so much that they become unrealistic.
- If the experiment is to be a comparison between the old and new capabilities, it is critical to also include the old capability in the pilot test to see if performance differences will occur.
- In a comparison experiment, design some experiment trials where it is expected that the old system should perform equivalent to the new capability and trials where the advantages of the new capability should allow it to excel. Both of these trials should be examined during the pilot test to assess these assumptions.
- New experimental capabilities that are to be simulated can be rigorously tested in the simulation prior to the experiment itself. The sensitivity of the simulation to differences between the old and new capabilities should be part of the simulation validation and accreditation. Pre-

experiment simulation of the old and new capabilities can also serve to identify trial scenario conditions that will accentuate similarities and differences between the old and new capabilities.

Threat 4: New capability has no opportunity to perform within a trial.

- Develop a detailed master scenario event list (MSEL) that depicts all of the scenario events and scenario injects that are to occur over the course of the experiment trial. These pre-planned scenario events and scenario inputs "drive" the experiment players to deal with specific situations that allow for, or mandate, the use of the new capability during the trial.
- Experimenters need to continually monitor not only that the MSEL occurred but also that the experiment players reacted accordingly. If the players did not attempt to employ the new capability when the MSEL inject occurred, ensure that the players actually "saw" the scenario inject.

TECHNIQUES TO COUNTER THREATS TO REQUIREMENT 2: ABILITY TO DETECT CHANGE

Threat 5: Capability systems vary in performance within a trial.

- For a single new capability system that has to operate continuously over the length of a trial:
  - Provide sufficient pre-experiment operating time for immature new technology to ensure that it will work consistently for the duration of an experiment trial.

- For an immature unreliable system, incorporate an experiment-fix-experiment methodology by designing a series of short experiment trials with treatment fixes occurring between trials rather than incorporating capability fixes (changes) during one long experiment trial. In this manner, the capability is held constant during each trial but allowed to improve from trial to trial in a systematic fashion. This experiment-fix-experiment experiment now has multiple, sequential capability levels that can be examined separately.
- For multiple new capability systems in a single trial:
  - Use the pilot test to ensure that all copies of the new capability function equivalently.
  - After the experiment, the experimenter can assess the extent of capability variability by comparing individual scores across items.
  - When variability is a result of a few outlier cases, the experiment analysis can be performed with and without outliers to determine the impact of outliers on the analyses.

Threat 6: Experiment players vary in proficiency within a trial.

- It is always best to deal with this threat prior to the experiment. Consistency among experiment player responses can be improved prior to the experiment by thoroughly training everyone to the same level of performance prior to the start of the trial.
- When possible, select similar (homogeneous) players to participate in the experiment to reduce player variability. However, this will compromise Requirement 4 (external validity).

- After the experiment, the experimenter can assess the extent of player variability by comparing individual scores across players.
- Variability in player scores can sometimes be statistically adjusted using covariance analysis with pre-experiment training and experience scores. Post-experiment statistical corrections are risky due to the statistical assumptions that accompany them.
- When variability is a result of a few outlier cases, the experiment analysis can be performed with and without outliers to determine the impact of outliers on analyses. However, keep in mind that "statistical" outliers may, in fact, be real impacts of the future capability and represent a serendipitous finding.

Threat 7: Data collection accuracy is inconsistent within a trial.

- When possible, use objective data collection measures that have been calibrated. Pretest data collection instrumentation to verify reliability (consistency).
- Questionnaire scales can be calibrated using techniques such as item analysis to quantify consistency indices, e.g. 85 percent internal consistency reliability.
  - Avoid binary responses and using continuous scales when available reduces data variability.
  - Increase the number of related questions about a particular judgment in a questionnaire and combine these related items into an "overall judgment score" to increase the consistency of the player survey judgments.
- Increase the objectivity (reliability, consistency) of subjective data collection procedures by adequately training data collectors. Data collectors can be objectively "cali-

brated" by comparing their observations across similar and dissimilar events during training.

- Consistency of subjective assessment across events is enhanced by having a data collector provide multiple component ratings (or scores) of a single event, and then using the component assessments to produce an average assessment score.
- A more consistent assessment can be obtained by combining or averaging individual assessments of two or more side-by-side observers who provide independent assessments.

Threat 8: Trial conditions fluctuate within a trial.

- An experiment result is more likely to be detected in experiments with a number of shorter trials with a constant condition during a single trial than having only one or two long trials, each having a wide variety of conditions.
- When the sources of the trial variability can be identified, some reduction in the variance can be accomplished by using statistical designs and techniques such as paired comparisons, matching and within-subject designs, blocking designs, and analysis of covariance.

Threat 9: Sample size and overall statistical power is low.

- Use an adequate sample size. There are available techniques for estimating sample size requirements to achieve specific levels of statistical power. In general, the larger the sample size is, the greater the statistical power will be.

- Accept more risk by setting statistical requirements lower, e.g. setting the statistical-rejection level at 90 percent risk instead of 95 percent. Setting too stringent of a statistical risk will not allow small positive results to show up as statistically significant.
- Use efficient statistical analysis techniques. Parametric techniques are generally more powerful than non-parametric techniques but they require more assumptions.
- Use efficient experiment designs such as matching, stratifying, blocking, or within-subject designs. Efficient experiment designs and statistical techniques can reduce the sample size requirement to well below the popular notion of 30.

Threat 10: Statistical assumptions are violated and error rate problems occur.

- Set the confidence level higher (e.g., 95 or 99 percent instead of 90 percent) to reduce the chance of incorrectly seeing a chance outcome as a positive change.
- Set the confidence level higher (e.g., 98 percent versus 95 percent) to reduce the chance of incorrectly detecting a false change in a large number of statistical comparisons in a single experiment. Increasing the required confidence level for each individual comparison decreases the multiple comparison error.
- Violating assumptions of statistical tests can increase the chance of incorrectly detecting a false change, but can also decrease the chance of detecting a real change. Analysis of variance is fairly insensitive to departures from assumptions of normality or equal within cell variances. Analysis of covariance, on the other hand, is quite sensitive to its requirement for homogeneous within-

group regression slopes. Non-parametric techniques, while less efficient than parametric techniques, require fewer assumptions than parametric statistics concerning the level of measurement and underlying distribution.

TECHNIQUES TO COUNTER THREATS TO REQUIREMENT 3: ABILITY TO ISOLATE THE REASON FOR CHANGE (IN SINGLE GROUP EXPERIMENTS)

Threat 11: Capability functionality increases (or decreases) from one trial to the next.

- Allow sufficient time for the pilot testing prior to the experiment to ensure the stability of the new capability functionality.
- Monitor that the functionality of the new capability does not change over the course of succeeding experiment trials where it is intended to be constant.
- When experimental systems undergo major modifications to functionality during a field experiment to correct deficiencies, consider whether trials conducted prior to the modification need to be rerun in order to make valid comparisons with the post-fix trials.

Threat 12: Experiment player proficiency increases (or decreases) from one trial to the next.

- Monitor for player changes over the course of succeeding trials. Players may become more proficient (learning effect) or they may become fatigued, bored, or less motivated. Player changes over time will produce an increase or decrease in performance in later trials unrelated to the new capability.

- Counterbalance the sequence of trials (e.g., NG-CG-CG-NG) so a sequential learning effect will affect the new capability group (NG) and the control group (CG) to the same extent.
- In general, conduct new capability trials prior to the current capability control trials. Any observed improvement for the new capability, when compared to the current capability, has overcome any learning effects.
- Ensure that players are trained to maximum performance and operate consistently prior to experiment start.
- Monitor for player attrition, which might impact trial results near the end of the experiment. When possible, compute each trial's outcome for only those players who completed all trials.
- After the experiment, analyze the trial data arranged by time to determine if increases or decreases in performance over time occurred irrespective of the nature of the trial. If temporal increases or decreases are found, analysis of covariance can be used (with caution) to statistically correct for unrelated temporal changes.

Threat 13: Data collection accuracy increases (or decreases) from one trial to the next.

- Continually monitor for changes in data collection procedures to ensure consistency.
- Re-calibrate sensitive data collection instrumentation before the start of each succeeding trial.
- Monitor for data collector attrition or data collector substitution after the trial has started. When possible, compute each trial's outcome for those data collectors

who completed all trials to see if their responses differ from those who did not complete all trials.

Threat 14: Trial conditions become easier (or more difficult) from one trial to the next.

- Exert as much control as possible over the trial execution conditions to ensure consistency from trial to trial.
- When new conditions occur that cannot be controlled, delay the start of the trial. When delaying is not an option, record the trial differences and report the estimated impact on the results.

TECHNIQUES TO COUNTER THREATS TO REQUIREMENT 3: ABILITY TO ISOLATE THE REASON FOR CHANGE (IN MULTIPLE GROUP EXPERIMENTS)

Threat 15: Experiment groups differ in player proficiency.

- With large treatment groups, randomly assign individuals different groups when possible. This is not possible when treatment groups must be organic units.
- With small treatment groups, use pair-wise matching when individual assignment to different groups is possible and when pre-experiment data on individuals is available for matching purposes.
- Use each group as its own control when random assignment is not possible. Each treatment group would use the new capability and the old capability.

- Avoid giving the new capability group extra preparation for the experiment, which would create artificial group differences (trained group difference).
- Monitor for differential player dropouts from the different groups over a long experiment to avoid evolving artificial differences between groups as the experiment progresses.
- Establish a "no treatment" control group when players are assigned to a particular experiment group based on low (or high) scores in order to offset "regression towards the mean," where players with initial low scores will show an improvement upon subsequent retesting, even if the experimental treatment is irrelevant to performance.
- Monitor for "dominator effects" in small experiment groups where one individual may drastically influence the group score for better or for worse.
- Monitor for "imitation effects" where one group will imitate the other group rather than respond to its own experiment treatment.
- Monitor for "compensation effects" (John Henry effect) where individuals in less desirable or more strenuous conditions will push themselves harder to outperform those in the easier condition. If the less desirable condition is the baseline control group, their over-compensation may equal any potential improvement in the new capability group.
- Monitor for "resentment effects" where individuals in the less desirable experimental condition may perform poorly as a result of being selected for this condition rather than the more desirable condition.

Techniques to counter threats to Requirement 3: Ability to Isolate the Reason for Change (in Multiple Group

Threat 16: Data collection accuracy differs among the experiment groups.

- Ensure that the new capability group does not get all of the best instrumentation and most proficient data collectors.
- The experimentation team, including the analysts, must continually scrutinize their own biases to ensure that their "experiment expectancies" do not bias the data collection and analysis.

Threat 17: Experiment groups operate under different trial conditions.

- Execute the trials for each treatment group simultaneously (same day, same time, same location, same targets, etc.) to the extent possible. Experiments of detection systems allow simultaneous presentation of targets to all experiment groups.
- When the different treatment groups cannot undergo their respective trials simultaneously, ensure that the trial conditions are as similar as possible (e.g., same day, same time).
- When simultaneous trials are not possible, counterbalance the trial sequence between two groups when possible (G1-G2-G2-G1) with Group 1 (G1) as the new capability group and Group 2 (G2) the control group.
- Monitor and report any differences in the experimental setting between groups.

TECHNIQUES TO COUNTER THREATS TO REQUIREMENT 4:
ABILITY TO RELATE RESULTS TO ACTUAL OPERATIONS

Threat 18: Experiment surrogate functionality does not represent potential future capability.

- Be aware of and report the strengths and limitations of surrogates and prototypes used in the experiment.
- Surrogates with major limitations are encouraged early in the concept development cycle for preliminary examination of the system's potential military utility, to help develop potential human factors requirements, and to influence design decisions. However, the limited capability to relate conclusions from prototype systems to production systems needs to be recognized and accounted for in later experimentation.
- Use fully functional prototypes when experiments are used as the final event to decide whether the new capability should be deployed to the operating forces.

Threat 19: Experiment players do not represent intended operational unit.

- Select experiment players directly from an operational unit that will eventually employ the capability.
- Use students, retired military, or government civilians when operational forces are unavailable and the experimental task represents basic human perception or cognition.

- Avoid the temptation to over-train the experiment unit to ensure success. An over-trained experiment unit is unrepresentative and referred to as a "golden crew."
- Avoid under-training by ensuring the unit is trained sufficiently to represent an experienced operational unit.
- Explain the importance of the experiment to the players and their contribution to the effort to ensure the new capability can be thoroughly and fairly evaluated.
    - Monitor to ensure participants do not under-perform out of lack of interest or resentment. This may occur when personnel are assigned to participate in the experiment as an "additional" duty perceived to be unrelated to their real mission.
    - Monitor to ensure players do not over-perform due to being in the spotlight of an experiment. This is known as the "Hawthorne effect." This effect is more likely to occur in highly visible experiments that have continual high-ranking visitors. In this instance, the players are motivated to make the capability look good to please the audience even though the capability may not be that effective.
    - Avoid inducing "experimenter expectancies" in the experiment groups where they perform according to the expectancies of the experimenter (also known as Pygmalion effect). If the experimenter expects the control group to do less well than the new capability group, the control group may perceive this and perform accordingly.

Threat 20: Experiment measures do not reflect important warfighting effects.

- Measure simple objective effects (time, detections, rate of movement, etc.) with data collection instrumentation calibrated for precision (non-bias accuracy) by pilot testing instrumentation prior to the experiment.
- Measure complex effects (information superiority, mission success, situational awareness, etc.) as a weighted or unweighted composite score of concrete components that can be measured objectively.
  - Measure the components of complex effects with alternate independent methods to avoid the "halo effect."
  - Measure complex effects with overall subjective expert ratings.
    - Estimate objectivity of subjective ratings through inter-rater agreement of independent experts observing the same event.
    - During training, have raters observe predetermined "good" and "poor" practice events to ensure that their assessments can differentiate.
    - Increase confidence in the subjective ratings by correlating them to independently obtained objective component measures.
    - Employ several raters independently and combine their individual scores into a single overall assessment.
    - The veracity and generalizability of expert ratings rest on the operational experience and credibility of the raters.

Threat 21: Experiment scenario is not realistic.

- Ensure realistic Blue force operations.
  - Develop realistic tactics, techniques, and procedures for the new capability prior to the experiment.
  - Allocate sufficient time for training the experiment unit in appropriate tactics with the new capability.
- Ensure a realistic scenario environment.
  - Identify the critical aspects of the capability's operational envelope, identifying those to be included in the experiment, and those that will not be included due to resource constraints or other reasons. This latter group is listed as "experiment limitations."
  - When particular operational envelope elements are believed to be critical to the success or failure of the new capability, these should be systematically varied in different trials so that the impact of each can be measured separately.
  - Approximate the noise, confusion, fear, and uncertainty of combat where possible. Allow the experiment to continue for many hours or days to generate fatigue-associated stress.
  - Allow for maximum free play and sufficient scenario space and events to promote player uncertainty, player creativity, and sufficient opportunity to explore and attempt to solve the warfighting problem.
  - Increase tactical realism of player participation by using lasers to simulate battlefield engagements.
- Ensure a realistic and reactive threat.
  - Conduct field experiments at national training centers when possible because they can provide realistic, well-trained threats.

Techniques to counter threats to Requirement 4: Ability to Relate Results to Actual Operations

- Use threat experts from the national agencies to assist in designing the "future threat" in the experiment scenarios and to monitor the conduct of the threat during experiment execution.
- Allow the threat maximum free play during the experiment to respond to and even preempt, if possible, Blue force employment of the new experimental capability.
- The development and employment of an intelligent, determined opposing force is one of the best counters to the threat of non-representative scenarios.

APPENDIX B

EXPERIMENT, TEST,

DEMONSTRATE, AND TRAIN

This appendix examines the similarities and differences among experiments, tests, demonstrations, and training. The discussion focuses on tests and experiments to demonstrate that there are many misperceptions about their differences and to show that they are more similar than different.

The overall comparison can be organized by reference to the prototypical experiment hypothesis paradigm: *If A, then B* and the follow-on question about A and B: *Does A cause B?* Figure 42 depicts how this hypothesis question is viewed from the perspectives of training, demonstrations, tests, and experiments.

Based on this paradigm, *training* can be characterized as practice with A in order to accomplish B. This is easy to see when B is characterized as a task with conditions and standards. The

Hypothesis: If (A) is employed, then task (B) will be accomplished.

	Event Goal	Event Purpose
Training	Practice on A to get B.	Operation to assist entity in acquiring the ability to do A.
Demonstration	Show how A works to produce B.	Operation to show or explain how A works.
Test	Determine if A works (produces B) -How effective is A? -Can the entity do A?	Operation to confirm the quality of A.
Experiment	Determine how B is produced. -Is A related to B? -How much does A affect B?	Operation to discover a causal relationship between B and something else (A).

Figure 42. Sorting Through Terminology

general task in the enclosed table is to detect targets. Task conditions specify the types of targets to be detected and the environment in which detections need to occur. The task standard might specify that 90 percent of the targets need to be detected to meet the training objective.

A *demonstration* is an event orchestrated to show how a process or product works. In our paradigm, it shows how A produces B. In the commercial world, demonstrations are used to convince prospective customers that a product produces its intended effect. In the military arena, demonstrations are primarily used as the initial step in a training event. The instructor will demonstrate the correct procedures to follow for A to produce B. Demonstrations are not used to determine if something works or if something causes something else. Product demonstrations are useful to convince others to buy the product or to illustrate the correct way to use the product. This is what tests and experiments do. Demonstrations assume that the product works. There is always embarrassment when the product fails to work during a demonstration.

TESTS AND EXPERIMENTS

In the military environment, testing is associated with system acquisition. Technical and operational tests determine if a system is ready to pass the next acquisition milestone. Acquisition testing can take many forms: bench tests, laboratory tests, chamber tests, and field tests. Warfighting experiments, on the other hand, are associated with concept prototype development. The purpose of this section is to clarify the similarities and differences between a test and experiment.

Terminology Confusion between Tests and Experiments

Our language promotes confusion between tests and experiments.

We conduct *experiments* to *test* hypotheses.

We employ *experimental* designs to *test* systems.

Both expressions use the terms *experiment* and *test* correctly. Random House College Dictionary (1982) provides the following definition for a test:

Test: the means by which the presence, quality, or genuineness of anything is determined.

Experiment: To explore the effects of manipulating a variable (from Chapter 3).

Tests determine the quality of something while experiments establish a causal relationship. The following two examples will illustrate the different purposes of testing and experimenting and that all experiments include the notion of testing.

A math *test* is given to confirm whether or not students have attained a certain level of math proficiency using the familiar letter-grade scale of A through F. A math *experiment*, on the other hand, has a different purpose than a math test. Math experiments are designed to explore something new, for example, to determine the best way to teach math. The primary purpose of a math experiment is not to assess each participant's level of math ability, but rather to examine the effect of different teaching treatments on the participant's math ability. During the experiment, a participant's math ability will be assessed (tested). The purpose of this test is to quantify the effect of the experiment treatment. The hypothesis of this algebra experiment might be: *If teaching methods (A) are used, then algebra scores (B) will increase.* One way to determine whether algebra scores increased is to give the students an algebra test before and after the treatment.

Similarly, the Army physical fitness test quantifies the level of physical fitness attained on a 300-point scale. A physical fitness experiment might explore two or more options for increasing recruit physical fitness. For example, one group of recruits spends additional time in physical sports of their choice while a second group spends additional time in organized calisthenics. At the end of recruit training, both groups take the same physical fitness test and their scores are compared. In this example, the physical fitness experiment is designed to determine whether the treatment (A), an increase in specific physical exercise, causes an increase in the effect (B), physical fitness. Again, a physical fitness *test* is used during the *experiment* to determine the outcome of an experiment *trial.*

Both experiment examples include the idea of testing. An experiment is a sequence of tests. Each experiment trial is a test of one experimental treatment condition. An experiment is a systematic sequence of individual tests to examine a causal relationship. A test is conducted to quantify a particular attribute.

Popular Distinctions between Tests and Experiments

One often hears warfighting experimenters caution their visitors: "Remember this is an experiment, not a test." Acquisition systems that do poorly in tests are in jeopardy of being cancelled. Undergoing an experiment has a different connotation. Tests include the idea of pass or fail. Experiments do not. Failure to produce a hypothesized experimental effect is more forgiving: "Let's try this and see what happens."

Another popular distinction is the misperception that "experimentation is messy but testing is precise." This perception most likely reflects the complex nature of warfighting: the chaos and uncertainty. Therefore, any experiments in the complex, messy warfighting arena must be messy. In one sense, this is correct. It is difficult to conduct precise experiments in the operational environment. However, it is equally difficult to conduct precise operational tests in the operational environment for the same reasons. Thus, while it is true that conducting military experiments in the operational environment is quite challenging, this is not a basis for distinguishing warfighting experiments from military operational tests. They both depend on the expertise and experience of the experimenter and tester to balance the requirement for a realistic environment against the needs to detect a change and to understand why the change occurred.

A third misperception is that "testing requires instrumented, precise data, while experiments use only high-level data." This

distinction would not apply to warfighting experiments conducted in constructive or human-in-the-loop simulations because
simulation outputs in these experiments are very precise and the
experimenter is often inundated with detailed second-by-second
data on every icon and action in the simulation.

This "data" distinction is most likely derived from the circumstances in which operational tests and experiments are
currently conducted in the field environment. Operational test
agencies have accumulated quite sophisticated data collection
instrumentation for use in field tests. When the acquisition
community needs to make a decision on a multi-million dollar
program, it can justify the development of sophisticated instrumentation to provide maximum information to the acquisition
decision. Conversely, experiments designed to examine the
potential of a new technology do not have the same incentive
to invest large resources in the answer.

Similarities between Tests and Experiments

It appears that any difference between an experiment and test
cannot be based on precision or quality data. So is there a difference? There are differences in purpose, but similarities in
execution. Part of the similarity in execution is the similarity in
language. Both activities conduct trials, collect data to address
measures of effectiveness, and issue reports. Moreover, they
both use similar "design of experiment" textbooks to design
their events.

If you fell into the middle of a warfighting experiment or an
operational test trial, it would be difficult to know which one
you had fallen into. In either one you would observe military
operators performing tasks to accomplish some mission. If you

	Target X	Target Y
New	12	16
Sensor	11	15
Current	11	12
Sensor	10	11

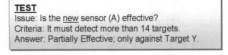

TEST
Issue: Is the <u>new</u> sensor (A) effective?
Criteria: It must detect more than 14 targets.
Answer: Partially Effective; only against Target Y.

EXPERIMENT
Issue: Does the type of sensor affect the ability to
            detect targets?
Hypothesis: If the new sensor (A) is deployed, then
            more targets will be detected (B).
Answer: The type of sensor impacts only Target Y.

Figure 43. Test or Experiment?

were particularly observant and could identify that some of the tools, equipment, or procedures employed were experimental, then you might guess "experiment." Nothing else in the event environment would indicate test or experiment.

It is only when the purpose of the event is known that subtle differences between tests and experiments are evident. As Figure 43 illustrates, tests focus on issues and criteria while experiments focus on issues and hypotheses. While this does not impact the basic design of the test or experiment, it does impact how the results are interpreted and reported as indicated in Figure 43. The idea of causality is central to both experiments and tests. The causal proposition is explicitly present in experimentation in the hypothesis; but it is only implicit in testing.

However, the logic of warfighting experimentation can be applied to military testing. If the test unit is not able to employ the new system, or if the tester cannot detect a change in performance for the new system, or cannot isolate the reason for performance differences to the system, or cannot relate these results to the operational environment, then the system test has validity deficiencies. While operational testing and field experimentation can be distinguished by their respective goals, they are quite similar in design, execution, and the four validity requirements.

SIMILAR RESOURCES
FOR TESTS AND EXPERIMENTS

Figure 44 summarizes the resources employed in warfighting experiments, operational tests, and military training. What is important in this comparison is that predominantly the same resources can be used for all three activities. This suggests that efficiencies can be gained if experimentation, testing, and training are conducted at the same ranges.

System Resource Requirements	Experiment	Test	Training
System Realism			
Simulation model	X	O	X
Surrogate	X	O	X
Simulator	X	O	X
Prototype	X	X	X
Operational system	X	X	X
Trained operators/units	X	X	X
Range Resource Requirements			
Instrumentation			
System-level diagnostic	O	X	O
Range interactions	X	X	X
Support simulation	X	X	X
AAR* feedback	X	X	X
OPFOR unit and equipment	X	X	X
Exercise control			
Observers/Controllers	X	X	X
Trainers	X	X	X
Analysts	X	X	O

* AAR = After Action Review

```
O = Not usually employed
X = employed
```

Figure 44. Resource Requirements

ABOUT THE AUTHOR

Rick Kass recently retired from a 30-year career in government service. This career included 25 years in designing, analyzing, and reporting on military experiments and operational field tests. Rick served 7 years with the Joint Experimentation Directorate in the United States Joint Forces Command (USJFCOM) and 18 years with the Department of Army Test and Evaluation Command (USATEC).

As a former U.S. Marine Corps Infantry Officer, Rick completed the Army Ranger School and the Navy SCUBA School and served with the 1st and 3rd Marine Reconnaissance Battalions. Rick is a graduate of the National War College and holds a Ph.D. in Psychology from Southern Illinois University.

Rick has authored over twenty-five journal articles on methods for research, experimentation, and testing. He was the primary architect for establishing a permanent Warfighting Experimentation Working Group in the Military Operations Research Society (MORS) and the past chair of this work group.

BIBLIOGRAPHY

Bacon, Francis. *Novum Organum*. Section 82. 1620.

Cebrowski, Arthur K. "Criteria for Successful Experimentation."
Memorandum for Secretaries of Military Departments. 7 July
2003.

Cook, T.D. and Campbell, D.T. *Quasi-Experimentation: Design and Analysis Issues for Field Settings*. Rand McNally. 1979.

Feynman, Richard P. *The Meaning of It All: Thoughts of a Citizen Scientist*.
Helix Books. 1998.

Kass, R.A. "Calibrating questionnaires and evaluators." *The ITEA
Journal of Test and Evaluation*. 1984.

Krepinevich, Andrew. "The Bush Administration's Call for Defense
Transformation: A Congressional Guide." Washington, DC:
Center for Strategic and Budgetary Assessments. 19 June 2001.

Myers, General Richard B. "Understanding Transformation."
Unpublished manuscript distributed electronically to students at
the National War College. 3 December 2002.

Owens, Admiral William A., U.S. Navy (retired). "The Once and Future Revolution in Military Affairs." *Joint Forces Quarterly.* Summer 2002.

Quadrennial Defense Review (QDR) Report: 2001. September 2001.

Rosenthal, R. *Experimenter Effects in Behavioral Research.* New York: Appleton-Century-Croft. 1966.

Rumsfeld, Donald H. "Transforming the Military." *Foreign Affairs.* May-June 2002.

Shadish, William R., Thomas D. Cook, and Donald T. Campbell. *Experimental and Quasi-Experimental Designs for Generalized Causal Inference.* Boston, MA: Houghton Mifflin Company. 2002.

Surowiecki, James. *The Wisdom of Crowds.* New York, NY: Anchor Press. 2005.

The Joint Staff. *Joint Vision 2020.* Washington, DC: U.S. Government Printing Office. June 2000.

INDEX

A

alpha error 62
alternate group 142
analysis 44
analysis of covariance 69, 166, 168
analysis of variance 166
analytic wargame 114

B

baseline 124
beta error 61
biased judgment 103
binary responses 67, 164
binomial probabilities 72
blocking 69, 166
Bonferroni correction 72
boredom 136

C

causality 20
cells 125
command, control, and communications 160
compensation 90
compensation effects 170
components 43
concept assessment 6, 152
concept discovery 151
concept refinement 5, 152
conditions 125
confidence level 72, 166
confounded results 41, 76
confounding 76
consistency 67, 101
constructive 114, 116
consumer risk 62
continuous responses 67
continuous scales 164
control group 76, 133, 140, 170
counterbalancing 80, 171

J

John Henry effect 90, 145, 170
Joint Warfighting Capability 6
Joint Warfighting Concept 6
Joint Warfighting Doctrine 6
Joint Warfighting Experiment 6
Joint Warfighting Prototype 6

L

learning effects 48, 81, 136,
    137, 167
lessons learned 4

M

Master Scenario Event List 56
maturation effects 48
measures of effectiveness 32,
    54, 59
measures of performance 32,
    54, 59
model-wargame-model 150
multiple-group designs 140
multivariate analysis of vari-
    ance 73

N

non-random assignment 141

O

objectivity 164
observer-controller 122

operational sequence diagrams
    121
operational validity 95
over-training 173

P

paired comparisons 69
parametric techniques 71, 166,
    167
participant motivation 90
pilot tests 53, 54
player attrition 82, 168
player dropouts 170
player expectancies 100
power 61
power analysis 74
precision 101
predictive validity 107
producer risk 61
prototype assessment 7, 153
prototype refinement 7, 153
Pygmalion effect 100, 173

Q

quasi-experiment designs 141

R

random assignment 86, 141
rational-deductive process 13
replications 48, 125, 126
requirements, validity 26
resentment effects 91, 170
rigor 23

Catalog of CCRP Publications

Coalition Command and Control*
(Maurer, 1994)

Peace operations differ in significant ways from traditional combat missions. As a result of these unique characteristics, command arrangements become far more complex. The stress on command and control arrangements and systems is further exacerbated by the mission's increased political sensitivity.

The Mesh and the Net
(Libicki, 1994)

Considers the continuous revolution in information technology as it can be applied to warfare in terms of capturing more information (mesh) and how people and their machines can be connected (net).

Command Arrangements for
Peace Operations
(Alberts & Hayes, 1995)

By almost any measure, the U.S. experience shows that traditional C2 concepts, approaches, and doctrine are not particularly well suited for peace operations. This book (1) explores the reasons for this, (2) examines alternative command arrangement approaches, and (3) describes the attributes of effective command arrangements.

Standards: The Rough Road to the Common Byte
(Libicki, 1995)

The inability of computers to "talk" to one another is a major problem, especially for today's high technology military forces. This study by the Center for Advanced Command Concepts and Technology looks at the growing but confusing body of information technology standards.

What Is Information Warfare?*
(Libicki, 1995)

Is Information Warfare a nascent, perhaps embryonic art, or simply the newest version of a time-honored feature of warfare? Is it a new form of conflict that owes its existence to the burgeoning global information infrastructure, or an old one whose origin lies in the wetware of the human brain but has been given new life by the Information Age?

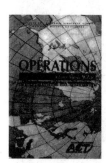

Operations Other Than War*
(Alberts & Hayes, 1995)

This report documents the fourth in a series of workshops and roundtables organized by the INSS Center for Advanced Concepts and Technology (ACT). The workshop sought insights into the process of determining what technologies are required for OOTW. The group also examined the complexities of introducing relevant technologies and devices.

CCRP Publications

Dominant Battlespace Knowledge*
(Johnson & Libicki, 1996)

The papers collected here address the most critical aspects of that problem—to wit: If the United States develops the means to acquire dominant battlespace knowledge, how might that affect the way it goes to war, the circumstances under which force can and will be used, the purposes for its employment, and the resulting alterations of the global geomilitary environment?

Interagency and Political-Military Dimensions of Peace Operations: Haiti - A Case Study
(Hayes & Wheatley, 1996)

This report documents the fifth in a series of workshops and roundtables organized by the INSS Center for Advanced Concepts and Technology (ACT). Widely regarded as an operation that "went right," Haiti offered an opportunity to explore interagency relations in an operation close to home that had high visibility and a greater degree of interagency civilian-military coordination and planning than the other operations examined to date.

The Unintended Consequences of the Information Age*
(Alberts, 1996)

The purpose of this analysis is to identify a strategy for introducing and using Information Age technologies that accomplishes two things: first, the identification and avoidance of adverse unintended consequences associated with the introduction and utilization of information technologies; and second, the ability to recognize and capitalize on unexpected opportunities.

Joint Training for Information Managers*
(Maxwell, 1996)

This book proposes new ideas about joint training for information managers over Command, Control, Communications, Computers, and Intelligence (C4I) tactical and strategic levels. It suggests a new way to approach the training of future communicators.

Defensive Information Warfare*
(Alberts, 1996)

This overview of defensive information warfare is the result of an effort, undertaken at the request of the Deputy Secretary of Defense, to provide background material to participants in a series of interagency meetings to explore the nature of the problem and to identify areas of potential collaboration.

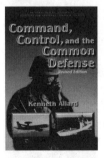

Command, Control, and the Common Defense
(Allard, 1996)

The author provides an unparalleled basis for assessing where we are and were we must go if we are to solve the joint and combined command and control challenges facing the U.S. military as it transitions into the 21st century.

Shock & Awe:
Achieving Rapid Dominance*
(Ullman & Wade, 1996)

The purpose of this book is to explore alternative concepts for structuring mission capability packages around which future U. S. military forces might be configured.

CCRP Publications

Information Age Anthology: Volume I*
(Alberts & Papp, 1997)

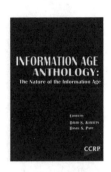

In this volume, we examine some of the broader issues of the Information Age: what the it is; how it affects commerce, business, and service; what it means for the government and the military; and how it affects international actors and the international system.

Complexity, Global Politics, and National Security*
(Alberts & Czerwinski, 1997)

The charge given by the President of the NDU and RAND leadership was threefold: (1) push the envelope; (2) emphasize the policy and strategic dimensions of national defense with the implications for complexity theory; and (3) get the best talent available in academe.

Target Bosnia: Integrating Information Activities in Peace Operations*
(Siegel, 1998)

This book examines the place of PI and PSYOP in peace operations through the prism of NATO operations in Bosnia-Herzegovina.

Coping with the Bounds
(Czerwinski, 1998)

The theme of this work is that conventional, or linear, analysis alone is not sufficient to cope with today's and tomorrow's problems, just as it was not capable of solving yesterday's. Its aim is to convince us to augment our efforts with nonlinear insights, and its hope is to provide a basic understanding of what that involves.

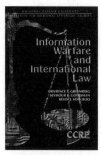

Information Warfare and International Law*
(Greenberg, Goodman, & Soo Hoo, 1998)

The authors have surfaced and explored some profound issues that will shape the legal context within which information warfare may be waged and national information power exerted in the coming years.

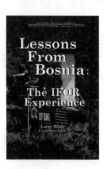

Lessons From Bosnia: The IFOR Experience*
(Wentz, 1998)

This book tells the story of the challenges faced and innovative actions taken by NATO and U.S. personnel to ensure that IFOR and Operation Joint Endeavor were military successes.

Doing Windows: Non-Traditional Military Responses to Complex Emergencies
(Hayes & Sands, 1999)

This book examines how military operations can support the long-term objective of achieving civil stability and durable peace in states embroiled in complex emergencies.

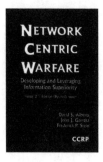

Network Centric Warfare
(Alberts, Garstka, & Stein, 1999)

It is hoped that this book will contribute to the preparations for NCW in two ways. First, by articulating the nature of the characteristics of Network Centric Warfare. Second, by suggesting a process for developing mission capability packages designed to transform NCW concepts into operational capabilities.

CCRP Publications

Behind the Wizard's Curtain
(Krygiel, 1999)

There is still much to do and more to learn and understand about developing and fielding an effective and durable infostructure as a foundation for the 21st century. Without successfully fielding systems of systems, we will not be able to implement emerging concepts in adaptive and agile C2, nor reap the benefits of NCW.

Confrontation Analysis: How to Win Operations Other Than War
(Howard, 1999)

A peace operations campaign should be seen as a linked sequence of confrontations. The objective in each confrontation is to bring about certain "compliant" behavior on the part of other parties, until the campaign objective is reached.

Information Campaigns for Peace Operations
(Avruch, Narel, & Siegel, 2000)

In its broadest sense, this report asks whether the notion of struggles for control over information identifiable in situations of conflict also has relevance for situations of third-party conflict management for peace operations.

Information Age Anthology: Volume II*
(Alberts & Papp, 2000)

Is the Information Age bringing with it new challenges and threats, and if so, what are they? What dangers will these challenges and threats present? From where will they come? Is information warfare a reality?

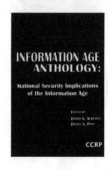

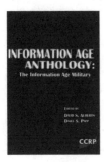

Information Age Anthology: Volume III*
(Alberts & Papp, 2001)

In what ways will wars and the military that fight them be different in the Information Age than in earlier ages? What will this mean for the U.S. military? In this third volume of the Information Age Anthology, we turn finally to the task of exploring answers to these simply stated, but vexing questions that provided the impetus for the first two volumes of the Information Age Anthology.

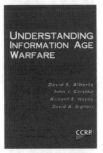

Understanding Information Age Warfare
(Alberts, Garstka, Hayes, & Signori, 2001)

This book presents an alternative to the deterministic and linear strategies of the planning modernization that are now an artifact of the Industrial Age. The approach being advocated here begins with the premise that adaptation to the Information Age centers around the ability of an organization or an individual to utilize information.

Information Age Transformation
(Alberts, 2002)

This book is the first in a new series of CCRP books that will focus on the Information Age transformation of the Department of Defense. Accordingly, it deals with the issues associated with a very large governmental institution, a set of formidable impediments, both internal and external, and the nature of the changes being brought about by Information Age concepts and technologies.

Code of Best Practice for Experimentation
(CCRP, 2002)

Experimentation is the lynch pin in the DoD's strategy for transformation. Without a properly focused, well-balanced, rigorously designed, and expertly conducted program of experimentation, the DoD will not be able to take full advantage of the opportunities that Information Age concepts and technologies offer.

Lessons From Kosovo:
The KFOR Experience
(Wentz, 2002)

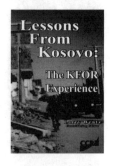

Kosovo offered another unique opportunity for CCRP to conduct additional coalition C4ISR-focused research in the areas of coalition command and control, civil-military cooperation, information assurance, C4ISR interoperability, and information operations.

NATO Code of Best Practice for
C2 Assessment
(2002)

To the extent that they can be achieved, significantly reduced levels of fog and friction offer an opportunity for the military to develop new concepts of operations, new organisational forms, and new approaches to command and control, as well as to the processes that support it. Analysts will be increasingly called upon to work in this new conceptual dimension in order to examine the impact of new information-related capabilities coupled with new ways of organising and operating.

Effects Based Operations
(Smith, 2003)

This third book of the Information Age Transformation Series speaks directly to what we are trying to accomplish on the "fields of battle" and argues for changes in the way we decide what effects we want to achieve and what means we will use to achieve them.

The Big Issue
(Potts, 2003)

This Occasional considers command and combat in the Information Age. It is an issue that takes us into the realms of the unknown. Defence thinkers everywhere are searching forward for the science and alchemy that will deliver operational success.

Power to the Edge: Command...Control... in the Information Age
(Alberts & Hayes, 2003)

Power to the Edge articulates the principles being used to provide the ubiquitous network that people will trust and use, populate with information, and use to develop shared awareness, collaborate, and synchronize actions.

Complexity Theory and Network Centric Warfare
(Moffat, 2003)

Professor Moffat articulates the mathematical models that demonstrate the relationship between warfare and the emergent behaviour of complex natural systems, and calculate and assess the likely outcomes.

CCRP Publications

Campaigns of Experimentation: Pathways to Innovation and Transformation (Alberts & Hayes, 2005)

In this follow-on to the Code of Best Practice for Experimentation, the concept of a campaign of experimentation is explored in detail. Key issues of discussion include planning, execution, achieving synergy, and avoiding common errors and pitfalls.

Somalia Operations: Lessons Learned (Allard, 2005)

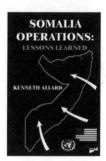

Originally published by NDU in 1995, this book is Colonel Allard's examination of the challenges and the successes of the U.S. peacekeeping mission to Somalia in 1992-1994. Key topics include planning, deployment, conduct of operations, and support.

The Agile Organization (Atkinson & Moffat, 2005)

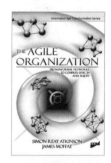

This book contains observations, anecdotes, and historical vignettes illustrating how organizations and networks function and how the connections in nature, society, the sciences, and the military can be understood in order to create an agile organization.

Understanding Command and Control (Alberts & Hayes, 2006)

This is the first in a new series of books that will explore the future of Command and Control, including the definition of the words themselves. This book begins at the beginning: focusing on the problem(s) that Command and Control was designed (and has evolved) to solve.

Complexity, Networking, and Effects-Based Approaches to Operations
(Smith, 2006)

Ed Smith recounts his naval experiences and the complex problems he encountered that convinced him of the need for effects-based approaches and the improved infostructure needed to support them.